Youth Ministry Advising
A Complete Guide

UUA Office of Youth and Young Adult Ministries

Carey McDonald and Jeremie Bateman, Editors

Unitarian Universalist Association of Congregations
Boston

Printed in the United States

Text and cover design by Suzanne Morgan

ISBN: 978-1-55896-682-6

6 5 4 3
19 18

This publication is a successor to *The Youth Advisor's Handbook: A Resource for YRUU Advisors* by Shell Tain.

Library of Congress Cataloging-in-Publication Data

Youth ministry advising : a complete guide / The UUA Office of Youth and Young Adult Ministries ; edited by Carey McDonald and Jeremie Bateman.
    p. cm.
Includes bibliographical references.
ISBN 978-1-55896-682-6 (pbk. : alk. paper) 1. Church group work with youth-Unitarian Universalist Association. 2. Church work with youth. I. McDonald, Carey. II. Bateman, Jeremie. III. Unitarian Universalist Association. Office of Youth and Young Adult Ministries.
  BX9856.Y68 2012
  259'.23088289132--dc23
                   2012021277

Contents

Supporting Youth Advisors

Creating an Advising Team ✐ Great Recruitment
Ideas ✐ Choosing Youth Group Advisors ✐
Training ✐ Contracts ✐ Youth Programs for
Our Future and Our Present

Resources

Youth Ministry and You

Youth ministry is the responsibility of every Unitarian Universalist. That's the charge that emerged from the multi-year Consultation on Ministry to and with Youth. From the Board chair to the Sunday morning greeters, from the youth advisor to the choir director, from the church staff to those who attend congregational events, all have a responsibility for creating space that recognizes youth as full, valued members of our communities and supports them as they engage with their faith. Choosing to serve as a youth advisor is one of many ways that adults in our congregations can demonstrate their commitment to youth.

Youth advisors fit a wide range of personality types, skill sets, and talents. The title itself can fit a number of different roles, and can include religious educators, ministers, and other religious professionals. However, all youth advisors should feel comfortable being an adult role model for youth, helping to mentor and guide them in your congregation. It's more than just making sure things run smoothly during a meeting. By serving as an advisor, you are part of a vision that calls for faith- and spirit-centered, multigenerational, multicultural, congregationally rooted ministry to and with youth.

How Did We Get Here? A Brief History

This vision of faith- and spirit-centered, multigenerational, multicultural, congregationally rooted ministry to and with youth didn't arise at random. It emerged from the history of youth ministry in Unitarianism, Universalism, and Unitarian Universalism.

Unitarian Universalist youth ministry has a rich tradition that dates back to the nineteenth century, when local youth "societies" on the East Coast came together to form the Young People's Christian Union (YPCU) for the Universalists and the Young People's Religious Union (YPRU) for the Unitarians. These early groups, focused on religious learning and social activities, held well-attended summer conferences. By the early 1940s, the YPCU and YPRU had transitioned into the Universalist Youth Federation (UYF) and the American Unitarian Youth (AUY), respectively, which were more centralized organizations with active national governing boards and regular publications. The AUY and UYF were frequent collaborators, holding their conferences and annual meetings together. In 1954, the two organizations joined to form the independent Liberal Religious Youth (LRY), predating by seven years the consolidation of the American Unitarian Association and the Universalist Church of America into the Unitarian Universalist Association (UUA). In fact, the creation of LRY is often recognized as helping to pave the way for the UUA merger.

LRY operated through the 1970s and became a cultural force within Unitarian Universalism. However, questions arose about the safety of LRY communities and LRY's governing structure, which resulted, in the early 1980s, in two continental conversations known as Common Ground. Young Religious Unitarian Universalists (YRUU) was formed in 1983 to replace LRY, along with a new Youth Office at the UUA to share responsibility for providing resources for districts and congregations, including the first edition of the *Youth Advisors' Handbook*. YRUU trained youth leaders to offer youth conferences in all parts of the country and helped to raise the voice of youth in national affairs, particularly through antiracism efforts in the 1990s. The YRUU national structure, known as Youth Council, was disbanded in 2008 to make way for a reenvisioning process. Although the continental organization YRUU no longer exists, the name persists as the descriptor of many youth groups and district-level programs.

Clearly, UU youth ministry has experienced numerous changes over time. These shifts have affected publications, staff support, governance bodies, conventions and conferences, and every other element of youth programs. Age ranges have also fluctuated, starting with the YPRU and YPCU, which considered youth to include members through age thirty-five. The UYF and the AUY counted youth as those aged thirteen or fifteen to twenty-five, and LRY's voting age range similarly ran from fourteen to twenty-five. YRUU's original age range was twelve to twenty-two, in an effort to better serve junior high school students, but the range was narrowed to a minimum of fourteen in 1989 and a maximum of twenty in 1992.

For a more detailed history of youth movements from their beginnings until 2005, please read *We Would Be One* by Wayne Arnason and Rebecca Scott, published by Skinner House Books.

Reenvisioning Youth Ministry

In 2004, a new chapter in youth ministry began when the UUA Board of Trustees convened the Consultation on Ministry to and with Youth, under the leadership of the UUA Administration and co-led by youth and adults. The Consultation engaged thousands of UUs in a reenvisioning process that would shape our youth ministry for the future. The Consultation found that although YRUU served some youth well, its scope and content failed to reach and to meet the needs of many other youth in our congregations. The Consultation also discovered that many youth sought increased spiritual depth, greater interaction with the rest of the congregation, a commitment to antiracism and multiculturalism, and opportunities for leadership at all levels of the denomination. In 2007, the Summit on Youth Ministry gathered together fifty youth and adults to translate the findings of the Consultation into a vision of youth ministry in which all youth are served and for which we are all responsible. The Summit articulated a vision of youth ministry that would be congregationally based, faith- and spirit-centered, counter-oppressive, inclusive and multicultural, and grounded in multigenerational communities.

This vision was then picked up by the Youth Ministry Working Group, a group of youth and adults tasked with recommending a framework and strategy based on the findings of the Consultation and the recommendations of the Summit. In 2009, after meeting for a full year, the Working Group released a body of recommendations for congregations, districts, religious professionals, and UUA staff that, if enacted, would bring to life the new vision.

The UUA followed the Working Group's recommendations and the vision articulated by the Consultation and Summit. It re-directed youth ministry resources to the local level and created additional opportunities, trainings, and events that would help youth take leadership in their home communities and get involved and integrated in leadership throughout the Association. This shifted the age range for youth ministry once more, focusing on "high-school aged or the equivalent for home-schooled youth," and re-orienting the definition from an age range to a life stage. The Working Group recommendations represent a blueprint for moving forward—including articulating the ways youth can and should be involved in congregational life and providing adults who work with youth with the resources they need. This report is available in full on the UUA website at www.uua.org/youth.

Today, youth ministry has developed a vibrant diversity of forms and expressions in churches, districts, camps, and regions across the United States. The UUA's Office of Youth and Young Adult Ministries remains committed to this new vision and works with districts, congregations, other UUA staff groups, individual youth, volunteer youth advisors, religious professionals, and others to bring engaging, relevant, multifaceted ministry to all of our youth.

The Vision in Practice

The vision that emerged from the reenvisioning process is both broad and deep. Here's what each aspect of the vision might look like in your congregation:

Faith- and Spirit-Centered

Youth enthusiastically called for the opportunity and the support to delve deeply into their faith. They want the opportunity to wrestle with important questions, deepen their own spiritual practices, and explore what it means to live their faith. This could take place in a variety of formats, including small group ministry, worship opportunities, or group conversation.

Multigenerational

Church communities remain one of the few structures in society that are not segregated by age. Youth value the chance to engage with other age groups in their community—and not just as the clean-up crew for the spaghetti dinner. Youth can serve on congregational committees, sing in the choir, participate in youth-adult religious education, teach children's religious education, or co-plan a justice or social action project with adult leaders. This vision reaches beyond the youth group, positioning youth as full members of a congregational community.

Being multigenerational is not just about youth coming into the "adult" congregation. It is also about adults who are not advisors coming into the youth community. Youth could organize and lead a worship service for the whole congregation, ask the Social Action Committee to partner with them on a project, or invite adults into their group space to share their stories.

Multicultural

A commitment to multiculturalism permeates the whole of youth ministry. It affirms a broad definition of multiculturalism that includes ethnic as well cultural diversity. Sexual orientation, gender identity, socioeconomic status, and ability (physical, cognitive, emotional/relational, developmental, etc.) all carry cultural markers and differences. Our youth ministry must recognize, affirm, and support youth with a plethora of identities.

Unitarian Universalist groups may be the place where a youth first feels comfortable coming out to his peers or where a youth of color isn't singled out for her difference. But this will be the case only if we've done the work together as a community to be welcoming and inclusive in our language, our assumptions, and our actions. This commitment has an outward focus as well, giving youth opportunities to understand privilege, power, oppression, and injustice, and to take action in their own lives and in their communities. Our youth programs can be places where youth of all backgrounds are welcomed, and can explore their identities, and learn how to work to confront racism and marginalization.

Congregationally Based

The crux of the shift in youth ministry was redirecting resources and efforts to support excellent youth ministry grounded in congregations. This means that youth advisors play an integral role in bringing this ministry to youth. Youth ministry at the district and national levels supports and enhances, but cannot replace, the role of the home congregation and a youth's primary religious community. When youth attend trainings and events, ask them to share what they learned with the group when they come back. Advisors who attend district conferences, rallies, and assemblies can bring back new learnings that will enhance their local ministry (see the section below on Cluster/District/Region).

Congregationally based youth ministry is important because congregations represent the vast majority of our religious spaces. Relegating our youth ministry and programs to places that operate outside our congregations sets our youth up to feel disconnected from the faith of their childhood when they become adults. This vision of youth ministry, by contrast, engages the gifts of youth before they become adults and allows our religious communities to be transformed by their presence. At its most basic level, congregationally based youth ministry is about recognizing youth ministry as part of our core mission as Unitarian Universalists.

Ministry to and with Youth

These prepositions are vital. We are called to minister *to* youth, and we are called to minister *with* youth. Youth ministry recognizes that youth need the support of their faith community *and* that youth have a myriad of gifts to bring to their faith community. They can teach, lead, and inspire us all. We must make room for them to do so.

What's Out There

There are many ways to put this vision into practice. Although this guide focuses on how to nurture the vision in your own congregation, here's a sampling of the larger picture to help orient you.

Local/Congregation

Each congregation's program uniquely meets the needs of its youth. Across the country, there are youth groups that focus on a series of projects for the year. Others spend Sunday mornings working through workshops and curricula, and Sunday evenings socializing and planning events. Some youth programs focus on small group ministry. You'll find youth serving on congregational boards and committees, as regular participants and leaders in Sunday worship, organizing with the Social Action Team, and teaching children's religious education. All of these actions put into practice the Youth Ministry Working Group's call for multiple pathways to involve youth in their congregation.

Cluster/District/Region

Like congregations, district and regional programs vary across the country. Some districts encourage clusters of congregations to host youth conferences (cons), while other districts host one large con for the entire area. Cons provide opportunities for youth to form community; share their skills, talents, and passions with one another; and deepen in faith. At the time this guide went to press, larger regions had also begun to collaborate on shared leadership trainings and other events. Summer leadership schools are increasingly popular and offer groups of youth the opportunity to receive in-depth leadership training over a longer period of time than a weekend training could provide.

In addition to trainings and other youth events, some districts have youth leadership bodies. Their function varies from district to district, but these groups of youth (and often adults) share some responsibility for youth ministry and conference planning in the area. They are often known as Youth Adult Committees (YACs) or District Youth Steering Committees (DYSCs). If you're new to an established youth group, you may already have someone in your group who is serving or has served on one of these bodies in the past.

Finally, districts may offer opportunities for youth to serve on the District Board or on another committee or task force. There may also be programming for youth at annual district assemblies.

To find out the best ways to keep up on all the opportunities available to your youth beyond your congregation, contact your district or regional staff member.

National

The UUA manages a number of resources to support congregations and districts in serving their youth. Your youth can also tap into national resources directly. The UUA's Office of Youth and Young Adult Ministries advocates for and supports youth ministry by connecting youth, empowering leaders, and equipping congregations. It also helps youth transition into young adulthood through the Bridge Connections program and other links with young adult and campus ministry groups.

National events include the General Assembly Youth Caucus, which provides youth-specific programming at GA, the Association's annual gathering and business meeting. Youth Caucus includes opportunities for youth from across the country to worship, network, and collaborate together. It is led by a team of youth and adult volunteers, allowing youth to take on a variety of leadership roles. The Multicultural Leadership School provides opportunities for youth and young adults of color to explore the intersections of leadership and racial/ethnic identity. Other UU groups such as the Unitarian Universalist Service Committee and the Unitarian Universalist United Nations Office regularly hold events that are geared for youth participation.

Resources

Throughout this book, you'll find resources to help you clarify your thoughts, organize programming, or simply learn more about youth ministry. Coupled with the rest of the information in this guide, they can help you find ways to create vibrant spirit-centered, multigenerational, multicultural community for your youth. Review the Resources section of this guide for more specific materials, and reach out to the UUA or your district/regional staff for support in finding the resources you need.

The Role of an Advisor

Congratulations! You've become a youth advisor! It's one of the most rewarding, if sometimes demanding, roles you can fill as a religious leader. If you are new to being a youth advisor, it may seem a bit overwhelming. There's so much to learn, and what happens if you make a mistake? Rest assured that every youth advisor starts out in the same position, and that your concerns are totally normal. This guide provides an overview of your role, common problems and strategies for resolving them, and ideas for how to create outstanding youth ministry. There is no one single way to be a great youth advisor. Your wrestling with how to strike the right balance as an advisor is a sign that you have the care and commitment it takes to succeed.

Advising youth can take many different forms. You could be part of a team of advisors that meets weekly with a local youth group. Or you might meet occasionally with the youth group as a support person for the group's advisors, as a driver on field trips, or as an extra adult for overnights and other activities. Some youth advisors teach a religious education course on Sunday mornings. Some work with junior high school youth, while others work with only high school youth. You might be a mentor in a youth group's Coming of Age program. Or you might be an advisor on the district Youth/Adult Committee or an advisor who attends district conferences.

Adults who know that working directly with youth is not the best role for them can still show their support for youth programming by advocating for youth within the congregation. Adult allies can contribute to a youth group's fundraising efforts, support a youth committee member's participation in meetings, flip pancakes at an overnight breakfast, or speak out in support of youth issues at your church's annual meeting.

There is no one path in youth advising. Some people first work with a local youth group, then find themselves volunteering for district programming, and later become involved nationally. Vary your experience to find the place that suits you best and to keep yourself from burning out.

Advising in a Local Youth Group

Advisors who work in local youth groups can have a wide variety of experiences. They might work with anywhere from two to more than twenty youth, with junior or senior youth groups, alone or as part an advising team of two to even five or six. Local youth group advisors might be supervised by the director of religious education, the minister, the Lifespan Faith Development Committee, a professional youth coordinator, or a combination of these leaders and groups.

The support and guidance advisors provide will vary based on the capacity of the youth with whom they are working. Advisors to a new youth group or a younger group of kids may find themselves leading most of the programming themselves. If the group has been around for a while and has developed strong leadership skills, then the advisor will be able to support the youth leadership that is already in place.

Advisors can find themselves volunteering anywhere from two to ten hours a week. Some will be reimbursed for their expenses or given an honorarium or salary, while others will not.

Congregations should support their youth advisors so that serving as an advisor does not result in any personal costs.

In addition to working within youth groups, advisors can also help their youth engage the whole congregation. From social justice projects to fundraising, committee membership to teaching Sunday school, the work of advisors should include advocating for youth among the adults of the congregation to help build multigenerational communities. Finding different ways for youth to participate in the congregation besides youth group can be especially valuable in small congregations where there are only a few youth.

Advising at Conferences and Events

Some advisors attend district conferences or national events, while others focus on local youth group overnights and excursions. Advisors who volunteer for regional events or district conferences will be involved with youth in a very different setting than those who only do local youth group advising. They will be making a two- or three-day, sometimes even a week-long, commitment to attend a conference with programming designed for youth. They may be asked to drive youth to and from the conference or to lead a workshop there. But unless you are one of the adults on the staff or planning committee for the conference, you will have fewer responsibilities than you will at your local events. Adults who are not on staff for the event are conferees; they don't have to run things. They are there to offer advice and support if requested and to respond in emergencies, but generally they are there to enjoy the experience as a mentor and ally.

Although it varies by district, like all other aspects of advising, the role of the conference advisor primarily involves modeling. An advisor goes to a conference to interact with youth, to be an adult who is not in a parental or authoritarian role, and to give youth a chance to relate to adults in an informal setting. For many adults, this can be a rewarding and rejuvenating experience.

Your sleeping arrangements and food will probably be quite different from what you are used to when you travel. You may find yourself sleeping on hard church floors or lumpy camp mattresses and eating vegan food. But conferences allow advisors to establish deeper rapport with youth. The conference experience is often more intense than weekly meetings. You will also have the chance to connect and share resources with adults from other congregations who are involved in youth work.

There should be an orientation meeting for adults at the start of each conference. If it is at your congregation, ask the youth on the conference staff to make sure that the new advisors are welcomed and included. And make sure that advisors are put in "touch groups" if they are part of the conference program. These are small groups of six to ten participants who touch base with each other periodically through the conference by playing games or engaging in other activities to help the group bond.

One of the biggest challenges for advisors who are new to conferences is connecting with the youth. It often helps to bring some activity that people can easily join in: Start playing your guitar or throwing a Frisbee, and you will quickly be surrounded by youth. Or bring a bag with crayons, markers, and coloring books. Find a table, spread everything out, and start coloring. Other artists will soon join you. Your shared interests or hobbies can be a path to meeting and making friends with youth.

Advising for a Larger Community

Adults who advise for district Youth/Adult Committees or other district youth governing bodies may find themselves attending monthly committee meetings and regular district conferences. These adults will be working with some of the most active and motivated youth leaders. They will often be asked to help other advisors in the district with ideas for youth programming and to function as a youth advocate in the district. Other responsibilities include serving as liaisons between youth and the District

Board of Trustees, the Religious Education Committee, the local UU Ministers Association chapter, people-of-color organizations, or other adult groups.

Some adults also choose to work with youth at the national level by attending General Assembly and serving on the Youth Caucus staff, or otherwise working with youth through national events or committees. These adults share their local and district experiences with youth and adults from all over the United States, and have the opportunity to establish closer relationships with some of the most experienced youth leaders from across the continent.

Qualities of a Good Advisor

Advisors must be at least twenty-five years old to participate in youth events organized by the UUA, and most districts and congregations have a similar policy. This has been the practice in youth programs for decades because it helps clarify the different roles of youth and adults, and ensures that advisors have appropriate distance from their own youth experiences.

Whether an advisor is twenty-five or forty-five, age is less important than how comfortable an advisor is as an adult. Advisors must be comfortable exercising authority and leadership within a youth group when it is called for, but they should not need authority and leadership roles to enhance their own self-image. Nor should advisors feel that they have to mirror the values and behaviors of youth in order to be liked. The integrity with which advisors articulate and act upon their own belief system is much more important. Advisors are models, not mirrors. The last thing youth want to see in an advisor is a reflection of themselves.

Advisors must also be aware of their own gender, racial/ethnic, and sexual/affectional orientation identities. In particular, it's important to be aware of the social dynamics associated with those identities. Given the call for youth ministry to include multicultural competence, advisors should receive training in these areas. Youth will be looking for mentors in this work and will need strong advisors to join them in exploring how marginalization works in our youth groups, our congregations, and society at large.

Advisors must maintain clear boundaries between themselves and youth, and sexual and emotional boundaries are paramount. Romantic/sexual relationships between advisors and youth are emotionally damaging, usually illegal, and unacceptable under any circumstances. Neither should advisors look to youth to meet their emotional needs. Just as it is appropriate for youth to look to their peers in the youth group for support with personal issues, advisors should look to their own peers for this kind of personal support. See the Creating a Safe Group chapter for more information on appropriate boundaries for advisors and youth.

Who you are when you are around youth is far more important than the specific tasks you perform. At a brainstorming session with youth and advisors at a district conference, participants came up with the following desirable advisor characteristics. A good youth advisor:

- Is fun, helpful, eclectic, sensitive, nurturing, drug-free, vulnerable, accessible, courageous, responsible, comfortable, a good listener, honest, flexible, genuine, interesting, neither evasive nor invasive, and tolerant of noise and mess

- Has a sense of humor, a great vision of Unitarian Universalism, facilitation skills, a strong sense of personal worth, an answering machine, and a solid sense of their own sexual identity

- Brings munchies

- Leads with a participatory style

- ▶ Sets personal limits

- ▶ Works well with others

- ▶ Helps make youth events succeed

- ▶ Wants to be an advisor

- ▶ Likes and respects kids as people

The same group brainstormed the following list of characteristics that don't work well in an advisor. A youth advisor should not:

- ▶ Be untrustworthy, uncommitted, a gossiper, condescending, undependable, needy, a couch potato, judgmental, opinionated, controlling, immature, a lecturer, without a vision, inflexible, negative, abusive, flaky, rude, or lazy

- ▶ Have unresolved issues from their own adolescent years, a private agenda out of synch with UU values, boundary issues, or a parental attitude

- ▶ Try to practice therapy on the group

Being a good youth advisor means being genuine with youth. This is difficult for many adults, who have often developed personas for effectively dealing with the world. In a youth group, youth are actively struggling to answer questions of how to be. They will challenge you to be vulnerable and real. You can help them see what it's like to be responsible, caring, and involved. You can show them by example what it means to be a Unitarian Universalist and to live out our values in day-to-day life. The youth you are advising are surrounded by adults who relate to them in the context of specific roles—parents, teachers, and other authority figures. You are giving them an opportunity to know at least one adult just as a person.

A youth group can go only as far as the youth leaders are willing to take it. Whatever your leadership style, you will always have more power than any of the youth in the group. If you expect them to be open and honest during a meeting, you will need to create a space for that to happen. You can do that by being open and honest yourself. Being who you are can give the youth permission to be who they are. Let them see how you handle mistakes, how you deal with your feelings, and how you handle conflict, while still maintaining appropriate boundaries. You want to be genuine and real with the youth, but always remember that they are not there to support you emotionally. Imagine that you have had one of those "weeks from hell." You come to the youth group meeting feeling frustrated and irritable. It won't work for you to pretend to be cheerful—the youth will see right through your act.

What will work is for you to be honest about how you are without asking the youth to either fix your feelings or join you in them. During check-in time you could say, "I have had a really frustrating week, and I'm feeling irritable, but I am ready to be here and hope to have a good meeting with the group." Enough said. You have been honest, vulnerable, and clear without asking the youth to provide you with emotional support.

Empowering Youth Leaders

As a youth group advisor, one of your key responsibilities is to promote youth leadership. If you do it well, you will find that you are not in charge of the group, because you will be sharing responsibility for leadership with your youth. This poses a dilemma, however, since parents and other adults in the congregation sometimes regard you as ultimately responsible for the group's actions—especially when things go badly. Having responsibility without direct control can cause anxiety. This can be assuaged by having confidence that even if everything goes against the plan, everything will ultimately be okay.

You can attain this balance by providing training for youth leaders and building trusting relationships between advisors and youth. If you actively promote a team environment of trust and accountability, you will create a healthy atmosphere in which the youth group members, with support from their adult advisors, can handle problems when they arise. When this dynamic is present, youth are empowered and feel free to act creatively—even whimsically—without making adults in the congregation excessively nervous. Review the Youth in Leadership chapter for a more in-depth discussion of the role of advisors in promoting and mentoring youth leaders.

Because this ideal state is hard to achieve and maintain, a youth group advisor must constantly reassess the balance between leading and advising. A youth group that has not yet learned to steer itself may need an advisor who is a more active leader. A group that has achieved what its members regard as the ideal state may feel squashed or disempowered if the advisor fails to recognize this and continues to lead too much. Remember, you are there not as a passive observer but to help the youth realize their vision and share their gifts. This requires you to constantly adjust your level of support to accommodate their evolving leadership skills.

Finally, a group that has achieved the ideal balance will lose it if it fails to pass along what it has learned to the next generation of youth and adult leaders. In youth group terms, a generation is every two to four years, and values and norms change with each successive generation. Working with youth groups is inherently cyclical. Constant turnover makes the youth group advisor's job tricky since an advisor's role may need to change from year to year.

Youth need to own their decisions and their consequences. Youth are full of energy, enthusiasm, and vision, but sometimes they don't know how to turn their ideas from vision into reality.

That's where you come in. If a group has never planned a social justice project for the congregation, they may not know what tasks need to be accomplished to pull it off. See if you can give this advice in a way that allows them to take responsibility for the tasks themselves, which will teach them much more than if they only watch you do the work. Ask them questions about what they're thinking or considering. And when youth complete a job successfully, they feel good about themselves and what they have accomplished. Your role as a mentor will help your youth learn the leadership skills they need to make the next project an even bigger success.

Moreover, adults who try to do it all themselves tend to burn out quickly. If you let go of the reins a little, you'll see how things can be different yet still work well. When the youth do most of the leading, you will be amazed at how creatively and competently they can pull it off.

Sometimes youth may fail, and you will have to rush in and pick up the pieces. At other times, when they don't follow through with their responsibilities, it may be appropriate to let a project fall apart so that they can learn from their mistakes.

Advisors must tread a fine line between rescuing the group all the time and letting members learn to live with the consequences of their actions. Experience is the best teacher of where that line is, but safety is the most important consideration. If anybody is in any danger, by all means, step in and straighten things out. You can always call a meeting once everyone is safe, ask the group members to take responsibility for what happened, and come up with a response.

Even if your leadership style is very collaborative, you are always a role model. Your tone and level of commitment will in many ways determine the group's complexion or attitude. Set a tone of interest and enthusiasm so the participants will be interested and enthusiastic too. If you are nonchalant, they will be as well. Groups whose advisors have a positive, can-do attitude accomplish much more.

There are a variety of resources available to assist with leadership development in your group. Contact the UUA or the district or regional field staff in your area for training opportunities. See the Resources chapter of this guide for more books and materials that can help you build a sustainable youth ministry program.

Parents as Advisors

Parents of teenage youth make some of the best advisors. They are among the most motivated adults since they have a strong interest in making sure their kids have a wonderful youth group experience. Whenever parents serve as advisors, though, it is important for them to get their teenagers' permission.

Sometimes children who didn't mind having their parents as advisors when they were young find the situation increasingly uncomfortable as they grow older. It can be difficult to open up and really be themselves with Mom or Dad there. When this happens, the parent, not the youth, needs to leave the group. A teen's youth group experience shouldn't be sacrificed for the advising experience of the parent.

If you have high school-aged children, please discuss the issue with them at length before you take on youth group advising. And check in with them periodically to make sure that it is still okay with them for you to be there.

The Advisor as Go-Between

Try as you may to encourage the adults in your religious community to interact directly with the youth, many adults just aren't used to relating directly to younger people. You may find yourself serving as a liaison between the two age groups, but you can be instrumental in breaking down the barriers between the generations.

Suppose, for example, that someone from your church's Social Action Committee calls you to see if the youth group would be interested in participating in a campaign to feed the homeless. First, applaud the Committee for reaching out to the youth in their congregation! You could ask your youth about the campaign and then relay their reaction back to the social action chairperson, or you could suggest that the chairperson speak directly to a youth in your group whom you know to be very interested in social justice. Better yet, you could ask the chairperson to come to the youth group meeting and talk with the entire group about the campaign.

In your role as a youth group advisor, you may also find yourself becoming an advocate for youth and for multigenerational community. When conflicts arise between youth and adults, you may be put in the middle. Your situation is often a sticky one: trying to educate adults on how to deal with youth as responsible individuals, while at the same time trying to educate youth on how to be responsible.

Because adults are in a more powerful position in our society than youth, it is difficult for a youth to disagree with or contradict an adult. If a situation arises in which you and other adults believe that the youth have made a mistake, try to build an atmosphere of mutual respect and understanding. Youth need an adult who can present the situation from their perspective while helping them to rectify the situation. Yours may be the only voice expressing their point of view.

For example, suppose your youth group requested the use of the church for an overnight. They received permission from all of the appropriate authorities, but the director of religious education gave them specific instructions not to use any of the supplies in the arts-and-crafts cabinet. The following Sunday, you find out that the director of religious education has banned all future youth overnights at the church because the construction paper, crayons, and glue were used. While talking to the youth, you learn that Rachel, who had been absent the day that the instructions were given, used the supplies because she didn't know they were off-limits. You recognize that the youth are still responsible for having used the supplies and that someone should have oriented Rachel to the rules.

The youth group comes up with a proposal to rectify the situation. They will raise funds to replace the supplies by holding a bake sale after church. They also promise that from now on, they will orient all participants at the start of all overnights. You and the youth make the proposal to the director of religious education, and even though he is reluctant to trust the youth again, you do your best to present the youths' perspective. If experiences like these are handled well, they will help build trust between the youth, staff, and other lay leaders in the congregation.

Creating a Safe Group

One of the keys to providing a space where youth feel comfortable to grow, develop, and express their Unitarian Universalist values is to have clearly defined boundaries and safety policies. The goal of creating these boundaries is not to guarantee that nothing will go wrong, but rather to model healthy relationships and protect everyone involved: you, the youth, and the congregation. Though it can seem daunting to handle the details of ensuring a safe and healthy youth program, remember that this important aspect of youth ministry must involve adults and, if done right, can help youth understand the value of healthy relationships for the rest of their lives.

Safe Congregations

Conversations around safety should be common for your youth by the time they reach high school, since, ideally, your church has crafted Safe Congregation policies for all situations, especially those related to children and youth. *The Safe Congregation Handbook: Nurturing Healthy Boundaries in Our Faith Communities*, edited by Patricia Hoertdoerfer and Fredric Muir, is available through the UUA Bookstore and offers a step-by-step guide to engaging the whole congregation in discussions about what it means to be a welcoming and safe community. It reminds us that paying attention to safety issues is a core ministry of the church because "our religious heritages compel us to address the important, widespread, and complex social issues of interpersonal violence and abuse. . . . When we gather in communities of trust and faith, we call that place holy ground."

Youth groups and gatherings can and do often model the "beloved community" that many adults seek. However, because minors have special restrictions and protections under the law, because youth are a marginalized group in contemporary society, and because youth are discovering and exploring the boundaries of relationships in their lives, youth advisors must feel comfortable discussing difficult safety issues and guiding the youth they serve toward healthy expectations. Youth advisors must also be prepared for occasions when youth cross boundaries and unfortunate situations arise.

Make use of the resources you have available when questions come up—or better yet, before they come up. Talk to your religious educator, minister, other advisors, or UUA or field staff when you need support. Check out the UUA web resources. Don't try to do it all alone! Advisors get themselves in trouble when they deal with unforeseen problems without the benefit of past experience or professional support.

Most important, the Safe Congregations approach involves the entire congregation to improve everyone's understanding of the importance of safe and healthy relationships. Youth groups are no exception, and engaging your youth in a critical discussion about safety is usually a more effective way to raise the issue than to simply hand down rules from on high. Youth should own the safety of their community, and your role as an advisor is to be a caring adult who both empowers them to address safety concerns and articulates the bottom line and associated consequences of violating the trust of the congregation at large. Help your youth form a behavioral covenant that is clear about expectations for sex, drugs, alcohol, smoking, confidentiality, and the way they relate to one another. Be mindful that gender-based distinctions include and affirm the full range of gender identity. Make sure your youth have the opportunity to discuss these issues at the beginning of a church year or event, not just when problems arise.

The following is the Policy on Sexuality and Community from the Participant Covenant, which is signed by all participants at UUA youth events (for the full text of the Participant Covenant used by the UUA for youth events, see the Resources chapter at the end of this book):

> While sexuality is a healthy and important part of young people's lives, there are times and places where sexual behavior is inappropriate. This policy seeks to create a healthy and safe space for all participants. Exclusive relationships detract from the community. All participants must abide by the following policies:
>
> ► Participants must respect each other's physical boundaries.
>
> ► Participants shall refrain from sexual, seductive, or erotic behavior while at the event.
>
> ► Sexual behavior between participants at the event and sexual harassment are not permitted and will not be tolerated.
>
> *Any harassment regarding race, color, national origin, religion, age, sex, gender, sexual orientation, or disability will not be tolerated. Such harassment includes unsolicited remarks, gestures or physical contact, and display or circulation of written materials or derogatory pictures directed at any of these categories. In addition, sexual advances, jokes, explicit or offensive pictures, requests for sexual favors, sexting, and*

other verbal or physical conduct of a sexual nature constitute sexual harassment.

The event leadership team is responsible for ensuring that this policy is enforced. Parents/guardians are invited to discuss this policy with youth.

Few things will make an advisor prouder than to watch a youth leader stand before a group of peers and speak with sincerity, seriousness, and eloquence about the importance of refraining from sexual activity while attending a UU youth event because of the damage it can cause to the beloved community. This is what a healthy culture around safety issues can look like in your youth group.

Good Practices

A large number of the safety procedures that could be considered good practice are common sense responses to the goal of avoiding any situation in which unsafe or inappropriate relationships could arise. Nonetheless, it is always helpful to carefully think through the details of how these situations work in practice.

Youth under eighteen should complete registration with the signed permissions of a parent or guardian to participate in regular youth and religious education programming. In addition to general contact information and information on special needs and preferences, this registration should include a medical release. Without such a signed form, your congregation may be held liable for accidents or injuries. Congregations should also have their legal counsel check parental permission slips for relevance to state/province and local laws.

If you go on any type of field trip or off-site event, be sure to obtain a signed parental permission slip specifically for that event for each youth who participates. Distribute forms to youth well in advance of any trips so they have enough time to get their parent's or guardian's signature.

Maintain an up-to-date roster of contact information for youth group participants, including email addresses and phone numbers. Make sure other church staff or leaders know when and where your youth group is meeting. Be sure to keep copies of contact information and medical release forms close at hand, including phone numbers for parents, guardians, and emergency contacts. Carry them with you if you are traveling from the church. We hope you will never experience an emergency during a meeting, but there are far too many stories of mishaps to take the risk of getting caught without this crucial information.

Make sure your congregation has developed a travel policy before taking the youth group on any outings. In many states, the church can be held liable for traffic accidents if the church provided transportation to and from events. This generally includes car pools if they were organized through the youth group. When creating a policy, consider the following questions:

▶ Does the church have a copy of each driver's license and insurance card?

▶ Is it okay with parents if youth ride in cars driven by other youth?

▶ Do you have a policy requiring drivers to follow all traffic regulations, use seat belts, obey speed limits, and comply with other safety issues?

▶ Do you forbid smoking in vehicles with youth?

▶ Do you have a minimum sleep requirement for drivers returning from overnight events?

▶ Do you have enough advisors or chaperones to provide for an appropriate youth/adult ratio?

Document any incidents or reports of injuries or accidents and keep them on file. Use a standardized form and make sure incidents are reported to the religious educator and/or minister of your congregation.

Another transportation issue often arises when bringing people home after meetings. Advisors should not be responsible either for taking youth home or waiting for parents to pick them up. If the meeting ends at 9:00 p.m. on Sunday night, it's unreasonable for you to still be there at 10:30 p.m. waiting for parents to show up. Try to make your expectations clear in your advisor contract. You should not drive youth home by yourself, since being alone with one youth in a car can be an uncomfortable situation and may be a violation of Safe Congregations policies.

Adults working with youth bear a special responsibility for monitoring their own boundaries and modeling healthy behavior. Congregations also have a responsibility to ensure that the adults involved in programs for youth and children do not have a record of violating those boundaries. Any adult working with youth, including youth advisors or sponsors at a youth conference, should complete a criminal background check.

In addition, stay up-to-date and informed on safety procedures. Ask your religious educator to provide training for youth staff and volunteers in basic first aid, child abuse prevention and reporting, universal precautions (handling bodily fluids and dealing with infectious diseases), and fire safety. Determine the process to be followed if there is an incident, disclosure, or accusation of abuse or neglect. Know your state and local laws on reporting abuse or neglect.

Power Dynamics

Your role as a youth group advisor brings a certain amount of power. Although you may find that power confusing or even unwelcome, it is unavoidable. You have power by virtue of being older and because you have more experience, knowledge, and financial resources than the youth in your group. Power is not easily defined or recognized, let alone embraced. It can be viewed in two ways: power over and power with. Situations of abuse are based on "power over," such as when a teacher gets sexually involved with a student, when a boss uses authority to silence employees, or when a spouse or parent physically or emotionally abuses a partner or child.

However, "power over" can also be used appropriately—as, for example, when a mother ensures that her child eats well and gets enough exercise. Young people have experienced "power over" in their relationships with their parents, teachers, and other adults and authority figures. This has been an important part of their learning and development, teaching them about who they are and how they are expected to act.

But for youth to grow into responsible adults, they need to start making decisions on their own. As an advisor, you have the opportunity to work with them in a "power with" model, in which you recognize youths' internal power, or "power within." "Power within" is the inherent worth and dignity that every individual possesses, which is expressed through their own ideas, opinions, feelings, and decision making.

Be aware that power relationships vary in each situation and context, especially in relation to categories of identity. For example, an adult male heterosexual European-American youth advisor has many sources of power in relation to a female lesbian Latina youth. It's important to understand the power dynamics inherent in your youth advisor roles and relationships.

Working in a model of "power with" encourages youth leadership and inclusive decision making. The "power with" model honors youths' voices. It helps them explore the ramifications of their behavior so that they learn to make good choices. It does not dictate to them what to do or when to do it but honors their choices—even if we feel they might not be the best ones available—as long as they are within a safe set of boundaries.

This doesn't mean that an advisor should never step in to use "power over" to influence youth. Like the parent of a child who runs into the road, you should step in anytime you feel the youth are in imminent danger and use "power over" to ensure their safety. For example, if during a worship service, the chalice accidentally set the curtains on fire, you would immediately grab the fire extinguisher and put it out. You would not wait for youth to explore their options, collectively try to recall where the fire extinguisher is kept, read the instructions on how to use it, and then put out the fire. Once the danger has passed, you can turn the event into a "power with" situation. The youth could brainstorm ways to ensure that this never happens again and decide how to make amends to the congregation and replace the curtains.

As the advisor, you are accountable for assessing the appropriate or inappropriate use of your power. Your age, experience, and the position the congregation has bestowed on you mean that you will always have more power than the youth. What you do with that power is your choice and responsibility.

Setting Personal Boundaries

Adults working with children and youth in the context of our Unitarian Universalist faith have a crucial and privileged role, one which may carry with it a great deal of power and influence. Whether acting as youth advisor, chaperone, childcare worker, teacher, minister, registrant at an adult/youth conference, or in any other role, the adult has a special opportunity to interact with our young people in ways that are affirming and inspiring to them and to the adult. Adults can be mentors to, role models for, and trusted allies of children and youth. Helping our children grow up to be caring and responsible adults can be a meaningful and joyful experience for the adult and provide a lifetime benefit to the young people.

Although adults must be capable of maintaining meaningful relationships with the youth they work with, they must also exercise good judgment and mature wisdom in using their influence with children and youth, and refrain at all times from using youth to fulfill their own needs. Young people are in a vulnerable position when dealing with adults and may find it difficult to speak out when adults behave inappropriately.

It may be difficult sometimes to stay in your role as advisor. The youth in your group are looking for a friendly advisor, but they still want you to be an adult. If you think becoming an advisor is a chance to relive your youth, think again. This doesn't mean that you can't play games or participate with your group. It does mean that you should keep a certain distance or boundary between you and the youth. They will not share with you at the same level of intimacy that they share with each other.

Additionally, if youth make demands or requests that are inappropriate, or are too physically affectionate with you, you need to set the boundaries. Be assertive. Ask questions; name the problem; state the consequences. Your comfort with maintaining these boundaries, using honest and direct language and making your voice and body language congruent, will enhance effective communication. Youth may be testing their own boundaries, but it is up to you to establish the limits.

When recruiting adult advisors, congregations should look for adults with a special dedication to work with our youth in ways that affirm the seven UU Principles. Good communication skills, self-awareness, understanding of others, sensitivity, problem-solving and decision-making skills, and a positive attitude are all important attributes. Additionally, leaders should have a social network outside of their religious education responsibility through which they meet their own needs for friendship, affirmation, and self-esteem. Leaders need to be willing and able to seek assistance from colleagues and religious professionals when they become aware of a situation requiring expert help or intervention. It is ultimately the responsibility of the entire church or conference community, not just those in leadership positions, to create and maintain a climate that supports the growth and welfare of children and youth.

At youth events hosted by the UUA, advisors abide by the following Code of Ethics included in the Participant Covenant. If your congregation hasn't asked you to sign this or another similar code of ethics, you should start the precedent yourself.

> Adults who work with youth are in positions of power and play a key role in the spiritual and identity development of younger members of the community. Therefore, it is especially important that adults be qualified to provide the special nurture, care, and support that will enable youth to develop a healthy, positive sense of self and responsibility. Youth and adults suffer damaging effects when adults become sexually involved with young persons in their care; therefore, adults will not engage in any physical, sexual, seductive, erotic or romantic behavior with youth. Neither shall they sexually harass or engage in behavior with youth which constitutes verbal, emotional, or physical abuse. In cases of violation of this code, appropriate action will be taken.

Any form of sexual relationship between an advisor and a youth is always inappropriate and can have legal consequences for the adult involved. This includes intimate physical contact, as well as verbal or emotional sexualization, such as flirting and sexual harassment. Youth are sensitive to the demands and innuendos of adults. Because they have rarely in their lives been given permission to say no to an adult, it's hard for them to do so. It is your job to put the needs and care of the youth first. If you hug someone and he feels uncomfortable or awkward, you have gone too far. Even if it feels to you like it's just an innocent hug, it doesn't matter: If the youth feels it's too much, it is. Here is a checklist of guidelines for physical contact between adults and youth, taken from the Safe Congregations Handbook:

- ▶ The touch is initiated by the youth.

- ▶ The touch is clearly not intended as a sexual advance.

- ▶ The adult does not experience the touch as a sexual advance.

- ▶ The touch is taking place in an open setting with other people around.

- ▶ The touch is clearly socially acceptable within the terms of the adult's advisory relationship to the particular youth, i.e., a handshake, a pat on the back, a moderate hug.

- ▶ The touch is something both the youth and adult can stop easily if it becomes uncomfortable.

Expecting the youth to fill voids in your life or help you through personal emotional struggles would render you unable to provide support for youth in that regard. We all derive benefits from working with youth; and for many of us, the work brings up some of our personal issues. This is normal. What you do with these feelings is what is most important: Your personal issues should not become the group's issues. Use your own network of friends, other advisors, the religious educator, and/or minister for support. If you feel yourself trying to meet your own emotional needs through interaction with youth, seek support and guidance from a professional staff member in your congregation who can help you strategize ways to avoid this dynamic.

Walk Your Talk

We all remember the old adage, "Do as I say, not as I do." It didn't work on us when we were young, and it doesn't work today. Whatever rules or behavior guidelines your youth group has set apply to you as well as the youth at all meetings and events. If the group decides on segregated sleeping at an overnight, you abide by that rule even if you are attending with your spouse or partner. If there is no smoking, you don't smoke; doing so breaks the trust and spirit of community you are trying so hard to create. You will come across as a good role model if you try to set the same standards for everyone, including yourself.

Advisors are granted the opportunity to develop a unique relationship with youth. You are in a relationship with them because you want to be. Remember that as an advisor, you are not a babysitter or the congregation's police officer. You are an adult mentor who offers help, support, guidance, and affirmation.

Communication

Confidentiality is important for creating an environment of trust and support in a youth group. This doesn't mean that you never tell the religious educator or parents what the youth group is doing. You and the youth group are, after all, a part of the congregation. However, it's important that you honor confidentiality by not talking about the personal events and feelings that individuals share with the group. It's fine to say that the group went on a picnic. It's not okay to tell people that Kevin, Crystal, and Maria got into an argument at the picnic about who had the most difficult parents.

As an advisor, you should set up regular meetings with your religious educator and/or minister. They should be kept aware of what is happening in the youth group so they can better support you and the group's programs. Youth ministry is a team effort, and no one should try to do it all alone.

And remember, while you want to protect the confidentiality of what is said in the youth group, you must also keep parents aware of what is happening with their children. They are invested in strong youth programming, or they would never have brought their children to be involved in the congregation. They can be among your best sources of support.

Schedule a meeting or send a letter to all the parents and guardians at the start of each semester to let them know what the youth group has planned for the coming weeks. If you need assistance in any areas, include a form at the bottom of your flyer asking for help. If you need drivers to an event, snacks brought for a meeting, or cookies baked for a fundraiser, find out what parents can provide. Building good relationships with parents helps ensure that you won't be left doing everything yourself.

Pastoral Care and Reporting Abuse

Your job is not to be a therapist but an adult advisor. Within that framework, you still want to care for and support the group and the individuals in it. In general, one of the best gifts you can give during a crisis is to make sure people have a place to talk about what's going on. When youth talk about tough or emotional issues, they often get nervous. They interrupt, they crack jokes, they try to divert the conversation away from the sensitive topic. You can help by encouraging them not to interrupt while others are talking and by bringing the focus back after a joke.

Be as honest and sincere as you can. Talk with your youth group about difficult issues like abuse, rape, suicide, intimacy, and trust. Provide them with resources such as the phone numbers for hotlines and the names and websites of youth agencies. Remember that your minister is always a good source of advice and counsel in handling tough situations, and will be able to offer pastoral care to your youth. Your minister can also help you determine when to refer your youth to human service professionals.

The issue of confidentiality can become a crisis for you as well as the youth when you believe or know that a youth is being abused. Learn the definitions of abuse (physical abuse, sexual abuse, emotional abuse, and neglect) and harassment. Be familiar with possible indicators of abuse—behavioral clues and other warning signs—and what various levels of disclosure look and sound like. You should be able to describe acquaintance rape and sexual exploitation, and to articulate respectful behaviors to help your youth reach the same level of understanding.

Every congregation should develop a procedure for reporting abuse and should train all church volunteers in these procedures. In most states, religious professionals are "mandated reporters," required by law to report instances of suspected abuse. It is important for you to know and follow the reporting procedures in your congregation and at any host community/site you visit with your group. Although youth group advisors may not legally be mandated reporters in some states, you nevertheless have a mandate to protect youth. If you know someone is in physical or emotional danger, you need to respond in a way that is best for that youth. If you have an established procedure and know your reporting obligations, you can develop clear statements that don't engage in denial, minimization, or blame, and that honor your responsibilities and accountabilities.

Let your youth group know the types of things you won't keep confidential. When you develop your covenant as a group, and the issue of confidentiality comes up, you could tell them, "If you tell me something that I feel indicates that you are in danger, I am going to have to tell someone else." In addition, every time your group starts a discussion in which confidentiality is named as a rule, remind your group of what the limits are.

If you do need to break a confidence that was shared in the group, you can pull that youth aside and inform them about what pastoral care avenues are available (talking with a minister and crisis hotlines, for instance). You may decide to say, "I know that when you shared your information, you asked that no one talk about your experience. But as your advisor, I am concerned that you are in danger. I feel I need to tell Reverend Mays about your situation. Would you like to go with me to meet with her?" By informing the youth of your need to tell and inviting them to join you, if possible within the context of the situation, you appropriately respond without leaving the youth feeling as though they are in a powerless position.

When you run into deep problems like these in the lives of your youth, remember to seek the personal and professional support you need. Getting the right kind of support from fellow youth advisors, religious leaders, and human service professionals can make all the difference both in appropriately addressing the situation and in making sure it doesn't come at the cost of your own stress level or legal exposure.

Unitarian Universalist Youth

Youth ministry in Unitarian Universalism is continually challenged to meet the needs of the current generation of youth. Young people coming of age today live in a very different world from the one most advisors knew during their adolescence. But they face similar issues as youth in earlier generations. They are going through tremendous changes, both physically and emotionally. Their ability to reason and comprehend abstract thought is developing in new ways, and the world around them is presenting ever-increasing challenges.

Youth experience tremendous developmental changes—physically, emotionally, intellectually, spiritually, and socially—in their teenage years. Younger teens are focused both on determining their own identity and their place within the groups to which they belong: Who am I in the world? Where do I belong? Which groups am I a member of? Who is the "us" and what do we believe? Who is the "them" and what do they believe? How do I behave to make sure I belong?

As youth reach their mid- and late-teens, they become more focused on individuation—more critical of the groups to which they belong—and look for ways in which they agree or disagree with the values and definitions of those groups: Do I really agree with what my family has always taught me about politics? Do I think my church's stance on transgender rights is correct? Is what my friends do really cool? What were once clear distinctions between "us" and "them" become fuzzier as youth grow increasingly concerned with carving out their own place and distinguishing themselves from others.

Youth also develop empathy for others as they learn to look at a situation from a variety of viewpoints. When they were younger, youth determined their behavior by how well it would be accepted by a group. Now they consider what is fair, just, and right. They begin to look outward to issues of community, politics, privilege, oppression, and social justice.

Teens often say they feel as if they don't fit in. They describe themselves as wearing a mask or just playing a part, or they feel they are not able to simply be themselves. Even if outwardly they seem to fit in and be accepted by their peer group, internally they may not be quite sure that they really belong. Acceptance is a frequent issue for all of us throughout our lives, but learning to feel okay just the way you are is crucial for a young person's self-esteem. As part of that acceptance, youth want to be recognized for their skills and special gifts; they want to be treated with respect and to be trusted.

Youth develop at different paces and in a variety of ways. The youngest member of your youth group may be the most mature. The most physically developed may act like the youngest kid. And don't be surprised when they change from one day to the next—the president of the youth group may act together and responsible when reporting to the Board and then behave like a silly goof-off the next day at an overnight.

Avoid assumptions about youth based on how they present themselves to you. The shy, quiet youth may be waiting for someone to offer her an opportunity to lead. The boisterous youth with lots of bravado may be faking, hoping for acceptance. Even though you may be working with only one age group, that group can be vastly diverse.

As they strive to grow and learn about themselves and the

world, youth seek opportunities to spread their wings. They need to taste adulthood and try it out. They want to prove their competence. Most of us remember adolescence as a time of struggle and discovery. Although what was happening in the world around us may have been a bit different when we were young, today's youth must choose their path, just as we chose ours. Youth today may confront issues at a younger age than we did, but essentially they are on the same journey that we took and that everyone must take.

Outside Issues and Pressures

As if figuring out who they are, what they believe, and where they fit in were not enough for our youth to deal with, our American culture presents them with many other issues and pressures: pressure from parents and school to succeed, and peer pressure on a variety of issues they will have to make choices about, such as drugs, sex, politics, smoking, alcohol, risky behaviors, and violence. Although we also dealt with most of these issues during our teen years, the level of exposure and intensity is stronger today. Youth are constantly bombarded with media images of violence and exploitation. Movies and video games are laced with violence, and the news media never fail to make sure that troubling incidents are always at the top of our consciousness. The prevalence of sexually transmitted infections and the increased availability of pornographic material have changed the way we address sex and relationships and have shifted our expectations about gender roles and sexuality, forcing our young people to face the most difficult dimensions of sexual behavior at a much younger age than in previous generations.

Youth look to their peers and adults in their congregations to help them face these issues and to make choices. Youth ministry can provide safe places to explore difficult topics. An intelligent decision is an informed decision, so youth need avenues for open discussion and support. Creating space for these discussions affirms the inherent worth and dignity of your youth and their personal journeys, and helps them pursue justice, equity, and compassion in our world.

Identity Development

Identity is one of the most basic and yet most complex dimensions of human development. Whether they are conscious of it or not, youth face a variety of identity issues. Some of these issues will be based on choice, while others (and this often comes as a surprise) may begin to emerge in a fluid, experiential setting.

In U.S. society, where rugged individualism is deeply rooted in our collective consciousness—and in our Unitarian Universalist culture that affirms the importance of each individual's personal journey—it is easy to believe that individuals determine their own identities. It is especially easy for youth to believe that they are wholly in charge of their own identities and their own decisions. And indeed, we do have a primary role in shaping who we are. At the same time, we form our identities in relation to one another, because identity groups are a social phenomenon. Part of who we are is determined by the groups we belong to and participate in, whether actively or passively. We simultaneously hold both a personal identity and a social identity. The two are inextricably related: Group membership is not simply tacked on to a person but is a real, true, and vital part of how we function in relation to identity groups. Individuals are shaped by social and environmental factors and by the culture in which they coexist.

Institutions also have identities, which may or may not be consistent with individual or group identities. While Unitarian Universalism is a pluralistic religion, it has a dominant—and very particular—cultural identity. As a facilitator, you may wish to explore (on your own or with the youth) the identity characteristics of Unitarian Universalism. You can then pay attention to which youth fit seamlessly into Unitarian Universalist institutional and cultural identity and which ones seem to exist in contrast to the dominant institutional culture. What are the implications for the youth group and how well it includes, welcomes, and supports all youth in the religious community? Identity is too important an issue for advisors to ignore. Take advantage of opportunities to learn more through reading and workshops.

A Welcoming Youth Group

A youth group is the perfect environment for encouraging youth to live out their Unitarian Universalist values by creating a just, compassionate, and affirming environment. This means creating a safe community that welcomes youth who identify their sexuality and gender in many different ways; youth from all types of families; youth of color and multiracial youth; youth with different physical, cognitive, and emotional/relational abilities; and youth from various socioeconomic classes.

Many of the youth in your group are probably exploring their sexual identity and gender expression. Note that sexuality and gender can operate independently, since gender describes one's own identity, whereas sexuality describes one's relationship with or attraction to other people relative to their own gender. For youth who may identify as lesbian, gay, bisexual, transgender, queer, and/or genderqueer (LGBTQ), UU youth spaces may be the only safe havens where they can be themselves and still be accepted. Referring to people in a gender-normative manner—such as by assuming that everyone is heterosexual by asking girls if they have a boyfriend and boys if they have a girlfriend—will convey a bias. These assumptions reinforce society's stereotypes as the only acceptable expression of sexuality or gender identities. It's safest to assume that there is at least one youth in your group who personally does not or whose family does not match those stereotypes.

Our society does not offer healthy images or role models for youth exploring their sexual and gender identities. Bring in films or books that are LGBTQ-positive and share them with your youth group. Have discussions that focus on sexuality issues and challenge any stereotypes or put-downs. Lead the sexuality education curriculum Our Whole Lives. (The Religious Education chapter provides more details.) Be seen by your youth as challenging unquestioned stereotypes elsewhere in your congregation. Offer to connect your youth with adult UU role models who have different sexuality and gender identities, and with whom your youth can identify. Invite these adults to speak to your group or serve as an advisor for conferences.

Our youth groups tend to be primarily white of European descent, but they are often more ethnically diverse than the adult population in our congregations. Youth of color in your group may be part of a family with two parents of color, one parent of color, or no parent of color. They may know only one parent. A significant percentage of UU youth of color are also adopted. In these cases, their parents may or may not be white and may be heterosexual or gay or lesbian. Youth of color and their families may be lifelong UUs or newcomers to our faith community. And there is an incredible range of terms that youth of color use to describe their identities: black, Latino/a, Hispanic, Chinese American, Chicano/a, multiracial, biracial, African American, Afro-American, Asian American, European American, Native American, mixed, Caribbean American, and Indian American, just to name a few.

These distinctions are meant to help youth leaders understand the dynamics at play and to recognize that the experience of youth of color, while different from that of white youth, is itself diverse. Evidence from the 2007 Consultation on Youth Ministry showed that youth of color tend to leave youth programs and UU congregations earlier than their white youth counterparts. This may be due to the alienating experience of being a youth of color in an environment that lacks mentors of color, a community of peers of color, or access to antiracism training for youth leaders. UU organizations like Diverse and Revolutionary Unitarian Universalist Multicultural Ministries (DRUUMM) may be of help; such organizations are committed to strengthening Unitarian Universalism's institutional ability to support and empower people of color in UU congregations and organizations.

One way youth leaders can support youth of color is to welcome and encourage questions related to racial and cultural identity. For many youth of color, including those who are adopted, racial/ethnic/cultural questions often come up years before they do for white youth. These questions are linked to their growing self-awareness, identity exploration, struggle against internalized racial stereotypes, and attempts to reclaim cultural identity and an individual sense of agency. Youth need to be empowered and supported in these feelings, and encouraged to keep moving along their spiritual path. Adult advisors of youth groups that include youth of color are strongly encouraged to network with groups like DRUUMM and the wider church to help strengthen relationships between youth of color and Unitarian Universalism. Youth group leaders may also want to invite guest speakers from the community or congregation each year to intentionally address the issues of race and racism. A conversation about racism in schools, for example, would be of interest to many UU youth. As an advisor, you can also help your youth of all races and ethnicities understand that their identity is never finished forming, and that it is a lifelong journey of becoming for all of us. Similarly, engaging with issues of racism and other social inequalities is an ongoing struggle that is a critical part of our faith as Unitarian Universalists.

Consider new ways to connect with communities of color in your area. This could include activities such as field trips to local ethnic restaurants, cultural heritage sites, and museums, combined with follow-up conversations about the experience. You also might explore, in conjunction with your church leadership, ways to connect with interfaith congregations and youth groups. As you make connections with local people of color and allies, you may find they are valuable resources to lead workshops at youth conferences. Youth exchanges with other denominations, such as the National Baptist Convention, Korean Presbyterian Church, African Methodist Episcopal Church, or other multiracial churches can be positive. The UUA curricula on interfaith engagement may be helpful in designing an experience with another faith community (see the Religious Education chapter for more information).

But be aware of racial inequalities of power that arise in developing these connections. Seek authentic relationships through long-term planning rather than short-term, feel-good activities that may be seen as token efforts. Look for ways to address the underlying issues of racism. You may find it helpful to involve UU organizations for people of color or other adults of color in your congregation who may have experience in facilitating these exchanges. Talk with your congregation's minister, religious education professional, or other religious leaders about how to conduct this type of outreach with integrity.

One youth group in Chicago developed an outreach program with youth of color from the area, opening up their group to youth from nearby shelters and group homes. They challenged adult members of their congregation to provide transportation to and from church, offer scholarships for youth to attend conferences, and become "big sisters, brothers, and grandparents" of youth who came to the church. This is just one way that UU youth groups can help congregations "walk their talk" around issues of racial justice.

In 2009, the UUA released the Mosaic Project report, which assessed the ministry needs of youth and young adults of color. Available for download on the UUA website at www.uua.org/youth the report includes recommendations for our denomination about antiracism and multicultural competency, multicultural community development, racial identity development, and communities for people of color. Other antiracism resources for all ages from the UUA include the Tapestry of Faith curriculum *Building the World We Dream About*, Jubilee Anti-Racism Trainings, the small group curriculum *Explaining Whiteness*, the JUUST Change consultancy, Social Justice Empowerment Workshops, and the multimedia curriculum *A People So Bold*.

The growing number of young people of color in our faith community continues to challenge us all to address issues of race, racism, cultural appropriation, and cultural identity. Your awareness of these issues is critical to helping our UU institutions create the systems and programs necessary to provide consistent and effective support for people of color.

Unitarian Universalist youth who are differently abled can also find a welcoming environment in youth ministry. Youth who are segregated in "special" classes at school and labeled as "different" by their peers can attend a youth group and be accepted for who they are. Make sure that any activities the group plans are inclusive of all members of the group. If the group wants to do a spiral dance for their worship, for example, ask them how they can arrange it so that the participant who walks with crutches can participate.

Don't make youth who have differing abilities take all the responsibility for advocating for their needs. Make inclusivity a goal for the entire youth group, so everyone is working for it at all times. See the Resources chapter of this guide for more materials to help make your youth group more welcoming.

Youth and the Congregation

As Unitarian Universalists, we seek to honor the gifts brought by youth who are blessed with a great deal of energy and the motivation to learn, create, and make an impact on their world. Congregations can benefit from the enthusiasm and passion that they bring to worship, social action, community outreach, and other areas of congregational life. Youth can serve on congregational governing bodies, be on a planning committee for the church retreat, lead religious education classes, be part of a Sunday service, and participate in the all-church cleanup.

Youth want to be welcomed. They want to feel part of their congregational community, just as adults do. If the only time adults invite youth to be involved in church programming is to do the dishes after the alliance lunch or babysit during the all-church potluck, the congregation is sending the youth a message that they aren't valued much. If that is the only message the youth hear, they may not want to stick around.

Youth should be an integral part of all church programming. They should be included in worship services, have representation within the church governing bodies, and participate in church fundraising events. Congregations that view youth as whole individuals and valuable members of their communities will help them develop into mature, self-confident Unitarian Universalist adults, while enriching the entire congregation. Building relationships across generations is rare in today's America, and church is one of the few remaining places where we can enjoy the fruits of a multigenerational community. Many congregations sponsor Coming of Age programs that help youth focus with their peers and adult mentors on some of the issues and concerns they have about growing up as Unitarian Universalists in today's world. See the Religious Education Programs chapter for more information on Coming of Age programs.

The age at which congregations permit a person to join and sign the membership book varies from congregation to congregation. Check with your society's bylaws to see what the age is for your congregation. When one signs the membership book, there is often a meeting with the minister, recognition at a Sunday service, a potluck with the Membership Committee, and/or a visit by a canvasser during the annual pledge drive.

Even though some youth may have been around the church since they were very young, their decision to join is no less monumental than that of the adults who are joining. In many ways, it is more momentous, since this may be one of a youth's first decisions to become a member of something as an independent young adult. It is, we hope, not a decision that has been defined for them by their parents, school, or peer group.

Many Unitarian Universalist churches balk at permitting youth to join the congregation. As member congregations of the UUA, churches have historically paid dues based on the number of people they count as official members. This money goes toward the operating costs of the Association and services to our congregations and districts. Churches have sometimes used this as an excuse to exclude youth from membership because most youth have little or no income and are frequently unable to pledge. In fact, many who are congregational members do pledge a small amount, which helps build a long-term sense of stewardship and connection with the church. When your congregation develops its membership guidelines, consider your congregation's values. Ask which is more important: your youth or the few dollars it would cost to recognize them as a valued part of the congregation.

Some states have laws that no one under age eighteen may vote on issues involving money. Several congregations have developed "associate" member programs that allow youth to belong and participate as every other member does, except that they cannot vote on financial matters.

Let's remind our adult members that the youth in our congregations are part of our multigenerational community. They may not meet on Sunday morning. They may be less visible than the younger kids or older members, but they are still an integral part of who we are as a religious community, and their contributions enrich us. Youth are also tomorrow's adult members. If we do not provide a place for them in our churches, they are less likely to remain Unitarian Universalists as adults.

Non-Unitarian Universalist Youth

Many local youth groups ask whether youth who are not Unitarian Universalists can attend and become members. These youth often come as friends of UU youth group members who want to share what they have found here with others whom they care about. If we don't reject adults who visit to see if Unitarian Universalism is something that fits with their values, then we shouldn't reject youth either. Please welcome and encourage all youth, Unitarian Universalist or not, who attend your meetings. These youth will still be subject to the same expectations about demonstrating UU values and receiving parental permission.

Youth ministry is about helping youth to become loving, caring, and competent adults. Many adults in our congregations came to Unitarian Universalism from other religious backgrounds. Some joined our denomination after their involvement in Young Religious Unitarian Universalists, or its predecessor, Liberal Religious Youth. Some parents join our denomination as a result of their children's involvement in youth programs. The values that youth learn in UU churches are clear; youth who do not share these values tend to go elsewhere.

Youth as Unitarian Universalists

Most youth in our congregations identify as Unitarian Universalists. They may not go to church regularly, especially if there is little or no programming for them there, yet they do see themselves as Unitarian Universalists. Youth groups across the continent vary as much as Unitarian Universalist congregations do, but UU values are consistent across our faith:

▶ Be respectful.

▶ Be concerned about each other's welfare.

- Be fair and nonjudgmental.

- Do not practice put-downs or demeaning teasing.

- Make sure that everyone is heard.

- Be inclusive.

- Be genuine.

Youth carry their identities with them into adulthood, including the identity of being a Unitarian Universalist. The values they internalize as UU youth inform their choices as adults about jobs, lifestyle, community, and relationships. In fact, there are plenty of young adults who may not be connected to any congregation or active UU community but still describe themselves as Unitarian Universalists. The formative experiences of so many UU youth have a clear lasting impact, and if our churches are able to harness this energy and vitality, we will have a bright future for our faith.

Youth in Leadership

The opportunity to grow as a leader is one of the most valuable gifts that youth ministry provides to young people. It benefits the youth, who are encouraged, supported, and empowered to take on responsibility and develop their leadership capacity. And it also benefits Unitarian Universalism, which gains strong, passionate, and prepared leaders in the present and for the future. Our youth ministry encourages youth to lead programs in their own communities and helps them gain the skills they need to succeed. It empowers youth to express what they think and feel, to learn to collaborate, and to live out their values in the world.

The opportunities for youth to lead vary widely and may differ from your expectations of what leadership entails. Advisors are integral in providing support and guidance as youth explore ways of leading in their communities and of making decisions in their group. This section will focus on how adults and youth share leadership in any youth program. The governing models presented in the Youth Group Nuts and Bolts chapter describe specific models you might use to help lead a youth group as an advisor.

Leadership Styles

The most recognizable leaders in our culture tend to be those in the spotlight. Whether giving a speech, directing a group, or orchestrating a large project, these people can be easily identified as leaders. They may be charismatic and confident in front of crowds, have a commanding presence, and communicate their vision and passion to motivate others. You will probably have youth in your group who exhibit this kind of leadership. They may already hold leadership positions in other organizations or at school.

You will also have leaders in your group, however, who prefer to be behind the scenes. No less passionate, dedicated, or capable than those who lead out front, these leaders may be quieter or harder to identify right away. They may step up to handle the logistics of an event or keep tabs on whether everyone is meeting their responsibilities. They may enjoy committee work or being part of organizing—but not necessarily facilitating—small group ministry. Although their contributions are essential, these youth sometimes go unrecognized. Everyone notices the youth who presented a workshop, but few might know who coordinated everything to make that workshop happen.

Additionally, you may have youth who are leaders in ways that few would recognize as leadership, at least in the formal sense. This form of leadership can be as simple as seeing a need and taking the initiative to meet it, unasked. It could be demonstrated by the one youth who goes out of his way to make sure the new youth group members feel welcome in the group by directly reaching out to them. Or it could show up as the youth who raises her hand during a discussion to ask the group to consider the exclusionary impact a decision could have. This sort of leadership by example is subtle, and the youth themselves may not recognize it as such. Nonetheless, it should be cultivated as much as the other forms of leadership.

These three styles of leadership are by no means mutually

exclusive. Some youth may be predisposed to one style, others may shift styles as their experience deepens, and still others may embrace all of them as required by the situation. The key is for you, the advisor, to recognize the ways your youth can be leaders and find ways to affirm their leadership and direct them toward opportunities for further growth.

Just as these styles are present within your group, to varying degrees at different times, they also exist among adults. It may be helpful to think about what your own leadership style is and how that intersects with your work with youth. Are you a take-charge, out-front leader? Think about how to temper your impulses as you lift up youth leaders into that role, so you don't overshadow them. Are you a behind-the-scenes organizational leader? You might need to trust the details to one of your youth. If your leadership is of the third, more subtle, variety, consider how to communicate your reasoning for an action or statement in a way your youth would understand.

Shared Leadership with Youth

Whether the group is nominally led by an advisor or a group of youth, the leadership will always be shared. The difference between these two approaches lies in the ratio of youth leadership to adult leadership

The Youth/Adult Shared Leadership spectrum on the following page illustrates how youth take on additional leadership as they grow in maturity, development, and leadership capacity. Note that at no point does one group completely eclipse the other; this is the essence of good shared leadership. Even in an advisor-led group, providing opportunities for youth to learn how to lead is essential. Conversely, in a group with tremendous leadership ability, the advisor is still part of the equation, checking in, supporting, raising difficult questions, and serving as a resource.

It's tempting to look at this graph and see a linear progression for your group, but that rarely happens. Your group may

Youth / Adult Shared Leadership

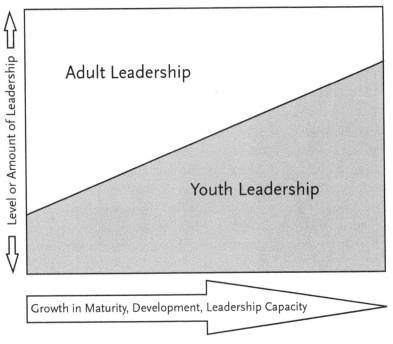

Level or Amount of Leadership

Adult Leadership

Youth Leadership

Growth in Maturity, Development, Leadership Capacity

be moving toward taking on greater responsibility for their own programming, but then a group of active youth leaders graduates, and the remaining youth with less experience need more direction. Or the group may have taken on more than they could handle and feel reluctant to have that much responsibility again in the near future. Shared leadership requires careful attention to where to draw the line between sets of responsibilities, and as an advisor, you should constantly reassess and reevaluate that line to ensure the right balance of support and challenge for your youth leaders.

One way to share leadership, particularly when your group doesn't yet have the leadership experience to handle an event on its own, is to assume the role of facilitator. Rather than planning, organizing, and running the event yourself, you'll model how to plan this type of event, effectively coaching your youth so they can do it in the future. In this role, you're neither spectator nor dictator. Your role is to guide the group. If, for example, the youth group is planning a service event, your role as facilitator is to guide the group through a conversation to decide what kind of project or topic they'd like to address. You help them sort through conflict, narrow their choices, and then make an action plan. You lead them through each step, involving them in the entire process.

On the other end of the Youth/Adult Leadership Spectrum, the youth in your group will be facilitating their own decision-making process. However, you still have a very important role to play as mentor.

Mentoring Youth Leaders

As your group takes on more leadership, you become more of a mentor or coach than a facilitator. In this role, you ask questions that get them thinking about perspectives they might not have considered, check in on how people are doing with their assigned tasks or in their particular roles, and intervene when necessary for the group's physical and emotional safety.

Youth Group Leaders

You'll work with your youth group leaders in a number of ways. One is to help spread the leadership opportunities around the group, which is important for a number of reasons. First, all your youth should have the opportunity to take on some leadership role if they so choose, which affirms our UU principle of the inherent worth and dignity of each person by honoring everyone's gifts. In addition, a few leaders holding all the power can discourage the rest and set the group up for trouble when those leaders bridge into young adulthood. Just as you are sharing power with your youth, you'll want to guide them to share power with each other.

You can also provide guidance when youth leaders need advice on how to handle a particular situation. A well-phrased question that gets them thinking about possible outcomes or helps them articulate what they're trying to say when they can't quite find the words can be more powerful than stepping in and making a decision. You may also be the one to raise an issue with them. You may notice that the leaders are becoming cliquey and excluding other youth. Or perhaps you've noticed a split in the group that the youth haven't picked up on yet. You'll work with your youth leaders to figure out how to proceed. Remember, this is a learning opportunity for them.

Youth Leaders in the Congregation

Although the focus has been primarily on youth groups, you will also serve a support function for youth who have taken on leadership beyond the youth group. Checking in with these youth about their experience on the Board of Trustees or on a particular committee can provide them with an opportunity to reflect on what they're learning or key you into any difficulties they might be having. For example, after such a conversation, you may need to serve as an advocate for a youth who feels that the adults on a committee are dismissive because of his age, and help him strategize about how to respond in a meeting. Or you may learn that serving on the Ministerial Search Committee has stoked your youth's interest in ministry, and she would like to find more opportunities outside the congregation. Youth who take on leadership in groups composed mostly of adults need support, both from peers and from allies. If you have a few youth serving throughout the congregation, consider hosting an informal get-together to chat about their experiences and build their confidence and comfort.

Leadership and Ethics

Helping your youth leaders understand the responsibilities that come with positions of power is another vital role of the advisor. You'll communicate this most often through example, just by being aware of your interactions with other people, even when you're not in an advising capacity. You can also help your core group of leaders or the group as a whole to think about the responsibilities that come with leadership. One of the more difficult things to understand—not just for youth—is how the role of leader sets you apart even when you're not actively leading anything. With the prevalence of social media, the fallout from a flippant comment to a friend or a photo that shows you breaking the group's covenant can be a serious point of tension. Perhaps your group will want to build expectations of leaders into their group covenant. Or perhaps your group of leaders will make one among themselves, highlighting the kind of leaders and role models they want to be.

Your role as an advisor also includes teaching your youth that the power that comes with leadership can be exercised in both ways that are healthy for the group and ways that are unhealthy. At UUA youth events where there are youth leaders and youth participants present together, all youth leaders are asked to sign the following code of ethics:

> Youth in leadership positions are uniquely visible and influential in any conference community. They are expected to recognize that power imbalances exist in their interactions with other participants. Sexual behavior with participants during the event is never acceptable; additionally, youth leaders should remain aware of the impact of their actions and behave accordingly. Youth who abuse their roles as leaders, consciously or not, can damage individuals and the community. Youth leaders are expected to use their influence in a positive manner.

What would a code of ethics for your group look like? If one is desired, develop it with your youth as a learning experience, rather than imposing it as a set of rules.

Coaching around Privilege and Power Dynamics

Advisors can be excellent mentors at helping youth foresee the effects of a decision. Advisors must be especially attentive and step in, either with a provocative question or with a direct intervention, when the group seems headed to a place that is harmful or exclusionary to youth from historically marginalized communities. That's not to say that your youth would intentionally do anything to harm someone in their group, but they can easily forget that their individual experiences are not universal or that something they see as benign could be hurtful to someone from another culture. These situations run the gamut from making sure that a member with physical limitations isn't excluded from the annual skiing trip to helping youth understand that costume parties in which participants dress as people from a particular culture can be hurtful.

Developmentally, adolescents may not yet be able to internalize the impacts of their social interactions on other people, even as they explore issues of universal justice, principles, and ethics. As you get to know your group, you'll get a sense of when a simple statement or question will inform their decision making and when you'll need to step in. When it comes to decision making, make sure that one group isn't dominating another and dismissing their legitimate concerns. More information on this topic appears in the Inclusive Decision Making section that follows.

Training

Support your youth by pointing them toward opportunities for leadership training. You might help your youth attend a district leadership retreat or apply for a summer leadership school, or you can advocate with the congregation to fund a small group of youth to attend a district event. You might serve as a sponsor so that your youth can go to General Assembly. You can learn more about leadership opportunities for youth by contacting the UUA or your district or regional field staff. District contacts are available at www.uua.org/directory/districts.

Recognizing Youth Leaders

Take the time to recognize the contributions of your youth leaders, whether in the youth group or in the congregation. If your congregation recognizes leaders and volunteers during a service, make sure that youth are included. Recognizing youth affirms that their contributions are valuable and appreciated. You can also encourage your youth to seek national recognition as part of the Luminary Leaders program. Luminary Leaders recognizes youth who have demonstrated outstanding leadership, networks them with other youth across the country, and provides opportunities for them to take on greater leadership roles. You can learn more about the Luminary Leaders program by visiting the UUA website at www.uua.org/luminary.

Inclusive Decision Making

By being inclusive, your group can undertake its decision-making process in a way that honors each person's gifts and concerns, and allows for effective decisions to move forward. The Chrysalis Program's Leadership Development Conference teaches the inclusive decision-making method. This program uses curricula provided by the UUA to offer training specifically designed by UUA field staff and religious professionals for their district or area.

Inclusive decision making combines the opportunity to share concerns and opinions, and to compromise in ways that help move past remaining disagreements, often through a straw poll or a vote. Some groups consider consensus the ideal form of decision making, but it can be difficult to obtain in a short amount of time. Alternatively, majority rule by majority vote is efficient but can leave members feeling unheard or silenced. Inclusive decision making is a compromise between those two forms of decision making.

The most important aspect of the inclusive decision-making process is that everyone affected by the decision has the opportunity to voice their support or concerns to the entire group and explore ways to address those concerns. Additionally, group members must be being willing to compromise or combine various ideas offered by group members. In doing so, members feel heard, understood, and willing to carry out the decision.

Inclusive decision making happens in five stages.

1. *Articulate the goal.* What is the goal? What, specifically, are we making a decision about? Background information about the goal will be needed so that all group members can make an informed decision.

2. *Brainstorm and evaluate options.* What are the possible options to meet the goal? What are the pros and cons for each option? List them where everyone can see.

3. *Name concerns.* Have each group member voice their concerns, which may be about particular options or about the goal in general. List them where everyone can see.

4. *Evaluate goals and options in light of concerns.* Is compromise possible based on the concerns shared? You may need to ask for elaboration on concerns. If so, reframe the goal and/ or options. If it is not possible to reframe the goal to the satisfaction of those with concerns, the group will need to decide how to proceed: a) not make a decision; b) use majority or super-majority vote; or c) return to brainstorming.

5. *Once a decision has been made, create a step-by-step plan to carry it out.*

   ▶ Articulate who is agreeing to what, when, where, and how.

► Set a timeline to complete tasks.

► Decide how to monitor or evaluate the decision (this may be its own decision-making process).

As an advisor, monitor the process. Is your group comfortable and honest enough with each other to share their concerns openly? If not, you may want to return to some group-bonding exercises or check in with individual youth about why they might not feel comfortable. You'll find more information in the Youth Group Nuts and Bolts chapter. You may want to prepare your youth facilitator for how to encourage open conversation and not shut down concerns. During the process, keep an eye on body language and whether concerns are being raised. If there are safety or inclusivity concerns that others aren't raising, raise them yourself. Finally, make sure that if a decision has been made by the leadership to move to majority vote, it isn't being used to silence a particular group of people with legitimate concerns.

Over time, many UU youth leaders become quite skilled in facilitating inclusive decision making. Ironically, this can lead to frustration and disillusionment for these leaders when they realize that the decision-making process in their congregation, school, club, or community is neither considerate nor respectful. As an advisor, you can help your discouraged youth find ways to bring those skills they learned in youth group to bear in making the world outside of youth group more inclusive. Show them how to advocate for silenced or marginalized groups, or how to address careless remarks in a heated discussion. Ultimately, Unitarian Univeralist youth will be ambassadors for our faith's values and principles, and they can use their experience in youth group as a platform for a lifetime of working to promote love and justice in our community.

Youth Group Nuts and Bolts

There is no one way to best run a youth ministry program, but this chapter offers some basic tools for creating a healthy youth group. These ideas will be helpful for groups just starting out, and can also help established groups to revisit the fundamentals.

Who Is Youth Group For?

In 2009, the UUA's Youth Ministry Working Group recommended the age range for youth as those in high school, considered to be grades nine to twelve or the equivalent for home-schooled youth. It is also important to pay attention to the groups immediately younger (middle school students) and older (emerging young adults), perhaps by finding ways to prepare future youth to join your group and by celebrating the graduation of high school seniors. However, keeping youth group limited to high school allows your programs to focus on that particular developmental stage.

Once your youth have left the high school age range and "bridged" into young adulthood, you will hopefully be able to remain in contact with them as an adult mentor. Maintaining connections with UU adults is one of the most effective ways to retain our youth as members of Unitarian Universalist religious communities after they become young adults. However, you should also be wary of including recently bridged young adults, who were youth group members only a few months before, in your regular youth group activities. Although returning to youth group may seem natural to them, these former youth can easily dominate the conversation and social space that belongs to the current youth. Events intentionally oriented toward both youth group alumni and current youth can be a more effective way of staying connected with your young adults. Visit www.uua.org/bridging for more information on bridging, including the UUA's Bridge Connections program, which connects former youth who have moved for college, work, or other reasons to a congregation in their new area.

Meeting Times and Locations

For both meeting times and locations, promote accessibility and predictability. The best location for a youth group to meet is a room in your church that can be used consistently. Ideally, this room will be designated exclusively for the youth group, allowing youth to decorate it and find a sense of identity there. The space you allot for youth group activity should be large enough for the projected number of members, and as always, should be accessible to people of all abilities. Taking care of this space should be high on the group's to-do list to ensure the congregation's respect and the group's continued use of the space. It is not generally recommended for youth groups to meet in advisors' homes because it puts additional strain on you as an advisor and can be inconsistent with Safe Congregation practices. See the Creating a Safe Group chapter for more information.

Choosing a time that is convenient for all interested youth and the group's advisors is crucial. Take into consideration the schedules of students, families, and advisors. Many youth rely on family members for transportation. The Sunday service is often a convenient time for youth groups to meet, especially for youth driven by people attending the service. Since parents, guardians, and other drivers will be at church anyway, it can work well, especially if transportation has been a problem in the past or travel distances are long. But there are disadvantages to consider as well. Youth group members and advisors are not able to attend the worship service with the rest of the congregation, missing the chance to learn to enjoy this style of worship, which is especially problematic if there is only one service. Also, the time for the group is limited to the length of the service and coffee hour, approximately one and a half hours. Sunday afternoon or evening is an alternative. Some congregations have Sunday morning as a structured curriculum time and Sunday night or a weeknight as a social and youth group business time.

You can help your youth group assess the pros and cons of available times and determine one that is best for them. Initially, keep the time consistent so that members can plan accordingly. Reevaluate after the group gets off the ground and, if necessary, every few months.

Communication

Establishing regular methods of communication is important, and only gets more important as the busy schedules of youth shift every year and sometimes every month. Be clear up front about how your youth leaders and group members expect to hear from one another—whether by phone, email, blog, or online calendar. This can also include expectations about responses, such as checking email regularly or following up on schedule questions within forty-eight hours. If you have business meetings, sending the agenda in advance will help your youth be prepared. You may need to be proactive about communication with your youth, but soon you can encourage your leaders to take over regular communication, which will allow them to build their skills.

Discussing communication will also help ensure that all youth have equal access to the information being shared in your group. For example, many youth groups find Facebook to be a great tool for organizing events and holding impromptu discussions. However, if some of your youth don't have access to a computer or have parents who don't allow them to use Facebook, the group should consider how to make sure they do not feel excluded. Perhaps you can limit Facebook sharing to topics that can also be shared by email. Check to see if your congregation has an online or social media policy as well.

Staying Flexible

Working with youth is often unpredictable. When you arrive at a meeting, remain flexible and open to change. Frequently things happen differently than the way they were planned. The person who was supposed to coordinate the meeting might be overwhelmed by the project or have other difficulties. You can refocus any confusion and disappointment by having or creating an alternate plan, perhaps in keeping with the same theme.

For example, suppose the group was planning to make plaster masks. Due to confusion about who was supposed to buy the bandages, you don't have the necessary materials. Instead, you might make masks from paper plates or paper bags. You might discuss masks, both real and psychological. Maybe you could make masks out of less traditional materials. What you don't want to do is focus on someone's failure. Use this opportunity to allow the group's creativity to solve the problem. But in case no one has any ideas, always come prepared with a grab bag of alternative activities.

Sometimes more important events change your plans. As an advisor, you need to stay alert for changes that may be more valuable or important to the group than the planned activity. Perhaps someone raised an important issue or personal crisis during check-in. Discussing the issue while it is fresh in everyone's minds may be of greater value to the group than the planned activity. Making masks can wait until next week. Regardless of the age mix in your local group, remain flexible.

Your group will evolve, it may grow or shrink, and your role as an advisor will change over time. Just keep a sense of humor and a dose of patience, and remember that with youth the journey is just as important as the destination.

Building Intimacy

New youth groups need to build intimacy and trust in order to work together, support one another in being themselves, have confidence in each other, and feel like a community. They can then focus their energy on the actions they want to accomplish.

Even if your local youth group has been meeting for several years, it will feel like a new group when you start with them. It will also be a new group after a summer hiatus or when new youth join in the middle of the year. Whenever you are involved in a group of any kind, taking steps to help develop intimacy and build trust will significantly improve the group's interaction.

Denny Rydberg developed a model for building intimacy in youth groups. He talks about the five stages that a youth group must go through in order to take action as a group: bonding, opening up, affirming, stretching, and deeper sharing. The following material is adapted from his book *Building Community in Youth Groups*.

Bonding

Bonding is the first stage in building community in a youth group. If individuals don't know who else is in the group, what they have in common, and how they are different, they will never feel comfortable enough to share, be supportive, and take action.

To bond, youth need to get to know each other. They need to start with emotionally low-risk activities that do not require them to reveal more about themselves than they are comfortable sharing.

Games or tasks, such as a scavenger hunt or cooking a meal together, are good bonding activities because they provide a goal and detailed instructions so that new members know what to do even if they have never been to a youth group meeting before. They also allow the youth to get to know each other in a non-threatening way. For example, if one of their first activities is making a display for the church fair, they can chat over papier-mâché about where they go to school and what movies they like.

Opening Up

This stage happens naturally as a group spends more time together, and superficial sharing about interests and hobbies deepens to discussions about hopes, fears, and dreams. You can facilitate opening up in your group by offering time for check-ins or leading games that require the youth to share a little more deeply about their personal concerns and opinions.

Affirming

As youth open up to each other, make sure that they always respond to one another in a positive way. As they start to share their personal ideas and feelings, hearing another group member say, "Oh, that's stupid!" will probably keep them from sharing again.

Remind the group that disagreeing is fine but that all are entitled to their own opinions, and that as Unitarian Universalists, we respect and honor a diversity of ideas. You can model this ideal behavior. If you continually affirm and support the youth and their ideas and efforts, they will be more likely to do the same for each other.

Stretching

A youth group "stretches" when it needs to respond to a situation beyond what usually occurs in its members' daily lives.

Opportunities for such stretching should occur after the group has bonded, opened up, and experienced affirming each other. Opportunities for stretching can be planned, such as participating in a ropes course or visiting a hospice for children with terminal illnesses. But they can also be unplanned, as when someone's parents get a divorce or someone is hospitalized after a car accident.

Youth groups that successfully face and respond to stretching moments tend to become very close as a group and work well together. Unfortunately, youth faced with a stretching experience before they are ready might be scared away by the intimacy of the experience. Whenever possible, try to introduce stretching opportunities only when the youth group has already progressed through the first three stages.

Deeper Sharing

Once group members have faced a challenge and successfully responded in a supportive way, they will be much more likely to share even deeper thoughts and feelings. They will be willing to take risks together, knowing that the community will support them in whatever they face. In this stage, youth will be ready to share their fears about coming out as gay; to cry about the betrayal they feel that a parent left them and has made no attempt to be in touch for years; or to celebrate the joy of a first love and relationship. A community that can share deeply with another in a supportive way is ready to take action.

If a new member joins a group that is already a tight community, then the group will have to back up to the first steps to bring the newcomer up to speed. If you are planning a deeper sharing activity and a new person is visiting, first have the group play a game or do a task together so the newcomer feels comfortable and connected enough to go on with the group. A new person will take less time to bond with a tight community than the larger community initially took to feel connected, but be sure to check in one-on-one with the new person after the deeper sharing activity.

In addition to trusting one another, it is paramount that the group learn to trust you as their advisor. This can only happen over time. Make sure you are very clear with your group about the kinds of matters you cannot keep confidential.

See the Creating a Safe Group chapter for more information about confidentiality and safe spaces. And don't forget that youth themselves can be a resource. The opportunity to discuss issues that are real and current is valuable for them and provides even more modeling for resolving those issues.

Covenants and Rules

When a group is beginning to meet or has just gathered again after a hiatus, work with your youth to create a covenant. A covenant is a mutually agreed-upon set of rules or guidelines about how a group will interact together. This shared experience proactively sets expectations for behavior and allows everyone to be on the same footing. Ask them: What are important qualities for making you feel safe in the group? How would you like to be treated as a member of this group?

Elements typically found in youth covenants include: no put-downs or hurtful teasing; one person talks at a time; and members should be on time. Many covenants also call on participants to be present and attentive during hard conversations. Finally, covenants often include expectations around safe behaviors related to confidentiality, drugs, alcohol, and sex. See the chapter Creating a Safe Group for more information on these issues.

Sometimes a small group may be formed out of the larger youth group for a specific project, such as a committee to organize a social action event. Even when everyone already knows and has formed bonds with one another, it is still valuable to help the committee clarify how it wants to act as a group for this task. What are the specific ground rules for this group? Are there any special considerations?

You and your youth group may have to develop other rules and guidelines, such as rules for a conference at your church or for a trip to Boston. Behavior rules and consequences will vary according to the traditions, expectations, and norms of the families within the congregation. Differences around issues like sleeping arrangements are common. Try to develop guidelines and rules that will lead to maximum safe participation in youth programs. Remember, the rules must be agreed to by at least four parties: the youth, the advisors, the church body responsible for youth programming (e.g., Youth/Adult Committee or Religious Education Committee), and the parents. Attention to these issues builds trust and safety. When youth and adults create and own the rules together, they lay the groundwork for mutual trust and respect.

The goal of rules is always to promote safety and community. Youth planning any event should establish rules in advance and in accordance with these principles, in consultation with adult advisors, and with respect for the concerns of youth participants and their legal guardians and/or parents. Setting expectations in advance is also far more effective in promoting healthy group dynamics than simply responding to problems as they arise. Adolescents are at the point in their development when they are seeking and testing boundaries, so making those boundaries clear will help them figure out what appropriate behavior looks like, and will also give you a precedent to fall back on if a youth violates the covenant.

When youth participate in multigenerational events, you may remind your fellow adults that behaviors that might seem commonplace to them can be viewed very differently by youth. Smoking and drinking are the two biggest examples, since both inherently exclude youth and potentially model poor choices. The impairment resulting from alcohol use or the social segregation of smokers can be barriers for youth who want to connect with adults in multigenerational settings.

At UUA-sponsored national youth events, both youth and

adult participants sign the Participant Covenant. (See the Resources section for the full text.) The Participant Covenant includes expectations around sexual behavior, an adult code of ethics, and additional rules specific to the event site.

Governing Models

The governing style that your group chooses may evolve over time. As the members of the group grow up and move on, the group's needs will change. It is a normal experience for youth groups to move through different governance styles over the years as youth leaders grow and gain skill, though all models retain a measure of shared youth and adult leadership. See the Youth in Leadership chapter for more information on the ways that you as an advisor can cultivate and support youth leaders.

Advisor-Led

With a new group or one composed primarily of younger members, you may want to start with an advisor leading most of the programming who can invite youth to participate, and then grow into one of the other models as the group matures. Remember that it's hard for youth to develop leadership skills if you continue to do everything, and advisor-directed groups tend to produce overworked, burned-out advisors. Although you may initially spend more time supporting a group that is learning to lead itself than if you simply did things yourself, the amount of extra time you invest in the beginning will pay dividends as the youth learn how to lead themselves.

Group-Led

This method can be challenging for both the advisor and the group. With this model, there is no specific structure or procedure for who does what. Every project or decision is undertaken in an ad hoc manner through consensus or acclamation, and specific leadership roles rotate. This style is simple and straightforward, but if no one in the group picks up the ball, a group project will fall back on the advisor. A small group may do best with this style. If, for example, you have only one advisor and six youth, working by group leading can be effective.

Elected Leadership

This is the traditional president–secretary–treasurer model— or, in youth group lingo: facilitator, scribe, and money manager. The drawbacks here are that quieter, more introverted youth may not feel able to participate or compete for leadership positions. The election process can also be divisive. But this style works in some groups. Traditional leadership roles can be efficient, educational, and supportive for an active group.

Youth/Adult Committee

This model works well with larger groups. The whole group chooses a smaller committee that is charged with carrying out the general plans agreed to by the group. Youth/Adult Committees (YACs) are made up of youth and adults, with youth usually being in the majority. Members share facilitation of the committee, and decisions can be made by consensus, acclamation, or vote.

One of the advantages of using a YAC is that you can involve more of the congregation's adult leadership in youth programming. The committee may have a trustee, parent, or former advisor as a liaison to the congregation. The religious educator and advisors can serve on the committee ex officio. This model is one of the most successful for long-standing local groups, both in terms of leadership development and accomplishing goals. In a YAC model, it will be important to pay attention to youth/ adult dynamics to ensure that both youth and adults feel they have equal voices in decision making and have the space in the discussion to share their best selves.

In certain congregations, the functions of a YAC may instead be folded into a Religious Education or Lifespan Faith Development Committee. These can be good ways of promoting multigenerational spaces, but broader committees that are also responsible for youth programming should make sure that youth are full participants and receive their fair share of support and group attention.

Groups of Different Sizes

The size of your group will fluctuate. Youth grow, change, and move on. You may have a very large group one year and a small group the next, as many of the youth graduate and move away. The departure of an advisor or changes in the congregation may also affect your group's size.

Change of any kind will affect the group. Some people will like it and some will vote with their feet. Although you want to provide positive ongoing youth group meetings or activities, don't be too concerned if the youth group isn't exactly the same as before. It is natural for groups to go through cycles, from large and active to smaller or even nonexistent. Just don't give up. Continue to support the youth you have.

Sometimes you will have meetings attended by only a few people. Planning for fifteen people and getting three can be disconcerting, but make sure you hold the meeting and make it valuable for the three people who do come. Focusing on those who don't show up will make the people who are present feel less worthy.

Also, small youth groups may give you the opportunity to experiment with new flexible structures. For example, if there are only three youth in your family-size congregation, perhaps your role as an advisor may be to convene a monthly lunch for these youth, to offer one-on-one support for finding other ways for them to engage meaningfully in congregational or district events, and to be an advocate and ally for them in the congregation.

When There's Trouble

One of the toughest things about being a local youth group advisor is getting support for yourself. This is a primary reason to team up with other advisors. If you reach out to other adults in your church for support, they may become actively involved with the youth program. The more adults who interact with the youth, the more integrated the youth will become with the congregation as a whole. Have regular meetings with your religious education director and/or minister if possible. If your church has a YAC, make sure you attend its meetings.

Regarding support, don't let your local youth group push you into cleaning up, taking minutes, or doing any other job that they don't want to do themselves. Make sure everyone helps with the hard tasks. As the advisor, you are still a member of the group. You need to make sure your rights are respected along with everyone else's.

Your youth group is a microcosm of the rest of the world—there will be the occasional crisis. Some problems will involve only a particular youth; others will affect the entire group. The support of your minister is valuable at such times. Don't hesitate to call for help; sometimes it's the most important way to support your youth. See the Pastoral Care and Reporting Abuse section in the Creating a Safe Group chapter for more information on dealing with these difficult situations.

Disruptive Youth

Every youth group seems to have at least one disruptive person: the youth who nixes everything, who interrupts or won't pitch in on any project, or who brings a lot of negative energy to the group—in other words, an advisor's worst nightmare. One of the best ways to deal with a disruptive youth is to build a relationship that will allow you to figure out and respond to their motivation.

It may be that the youth doesn't want to be in the group but is being forced to attend by a parent. If that is the case, find out where the youth would rather be. He might be fascinated by toddlers and would like to help in the nursery. Maybe she wants to work with the sexton setting up coffee hour and fixing things around the church.

Some disruptive youth are just hungry for leadership opportunities they have never had. If you can channel their negative leadership in a positive direction, you will have a tremendous ally in the group. Don't forget to hold your youth accountable to the covenant they have made with each other and ask them to be responsible for responding to any breaches.

In one church, a youth was so disruptive that he was told not to attend the youth group for the quarter. The minister asked him where in the church he would like to be involved on Sunday mornings. The boy thought that setting up the church bookstore for coffee hour seemed interesting, so he started working with the person who handled the bookstore. He never rejoined the youth group, but after a year or two he was the head of the bookstore, doing all the accounting and book ordering.

Of course, behavioral problems are sometimes the sign of deeper concerns in the life of your high school youth, concerns that go beyond normal adolescent development. If you have built a good relationship with your youth over the years, you may be able to get a sense of whether something more significant than discomfort or frustration with the group is at play, such as depression, addiction, or emotional trauma. Again, when your youth are encountering problems that require more than a sympathetic ear and affirmation, reach out to the religious professionals in your congregation or district.

Finally, be careful not to pigeonhole youth. Your most disruptive youth one year may turn out to be your most dynamic leader the next. Youth grow and change constantly, so give them the benefit of the doubt. You are most likely to get mature behavior from them if you always expect it. Despite the fact that they regularly rise to the occasion and meet our high expectations, we seem to be somehow surprised when it happens. In fact, situations in which our youth grow and mature right before our eyes can be some of the most rewarding for an advisor.

Creating a Balanced Program

Youth ministry has many dimensions, and a successful youth program will include a balance of elements. As an advisor, you should encourage the youth to incorporate all the elements discussed in this chapter into their program, recognizing that they may need more of one or another at different times. For example, a new or younger youth group will need more time for building community until members feel bonded. Youth groups are generally not willing to worship together until they feel comfortable with each other. It is also important to realize that almost any activity has elements of more than one component. This chapter describes these elements using two models: the Six Pillars of Balanced Youth Programs and the Web of Youth Ministry. Check out the Project Ideas in the Resources section for examples of how groups can integrate these elements into specific projects.

The Six Pillars of Balanced Youth Programs

This model is well known in circles of youth advisors. The pillars consist of six aspects of effective youth ministry: Building Community, Social Action, Worship, Learning, Leadership, and Congregational Involvement.

Building Community

Community building, or socializing, is time for people to get to know one another—time devoted to hanging out. Nothing can be accomplished until people know, trust, and care about each other and the group's success. Sometimes advisors tend to minimize the community-building or social component of youth groups, or think that youth groups should have exclusively educational and worshipful activities. Yet some of the most valuable experiences for youth happen during social activities. This time is for bonding, sharing values, establishing trust, generating intimacy, and practicing acceptance.

Building this type of community allows Unitarian Universalist youth to share their values. And the community they build here can help sustain and support them in their social interactions outside of UU situations. The rest of your congregation places an emphasis on the social element of their programs—imagine if there were no coffee hour, potluck dinners, fairs, or retreats. Make sure the youth have the same opportunities to socialize within their community. Youth group is often one of the few places that youth have for simply being together. School, religious education programs, and after-school sports or music lessons are all highly structured activities. Even when the youth group is involved with a more structured project, offer them some unscheduled time, perhaps a half-hour gathering before or after the meeting. You can also try the following activities:

Game Night   Have group members bring board games or play physical games like tag or hide-and-seek. There are games that create space for sharing, such as "two truths and a lie." In that game, each person takes a turn describing two truths and one lie about themselves, and the rest of the group has to guess which is the lie. You can learn surprising things about people with games like this.

Movie Night   Let the youth pick the movie, but be sure it has a rating appropriate for the group. Have youth bring sleeping bags and pillows. They might come to the meeting in their pajamas or dressed in theme outfits in keeping with the movie. Allow time to talk about the movie; even comedies generate opinions. Don't forget the popcorn.

Parties   Theme parties are wonderful icebreakers. Youth can really get into dressing up or creating unique menus.

Outings   Take your group on a picnic or camping trip, or you can go to the beach, a swimming pool, or a museum. Remember to be sensitive to the economic situations and physical abilities of the individuals in the group. Although hiking trips can be wonderful, please be aware of youth who may not be able to participate in these events for financial or ability reasons. You don't want anyone to feel excluded. If it wants to, your group can raise the funds to make more expensive events possible. Bake sales or car washes can be enjoyable community-building events as well as fundraisers.

Watch for power dynamics due to gender, race, class, ability, or sexual orientation. During social events, many of our youth feel limited in their ability to participate because their voices are drowned out by those from more privileged or established backgrounds. Youth advisors can monitor this situation and help youth take part more fully. See the chapter Youth in Leadership for more information on coaching in these situations.

Social Action

Engaging with social justice issues is one of the main ways Unitarian Universalists express our faith in the world, and youth are often at the forefront of this expression. Social action can be exciting, challenging, and rewarding, whether based on a single project or long-term engagement with an issue.

Social justice action takes many forms because it involves so many interrelated people, groups, and issues. Although we may traditionally think of social action as being limited to service (e.g., volunteering at a soup kitchen) or witness (e.g., participating in a protest march), these are only two of the five approaches. These approaches, adapted from the UUA's Social Justice Empowerment Handbook for Congregations, can help youth realize their desire to impact their community:

Service   Our ability to meet the needs of persons in distress

Examples: collecting money, donating food or clothing, tutoring, sheltering the homeless, helping senior citizens, providing childcare

Education   Learning about the importance and context of a social issue, and interpreting the issue within the context of liberal religious values

Examples: public meetings, workshops, resolutions, drama, public forums, worship services, and sermons

Witness   Making a public statement through word or action based on convictions regarding a particular issue

Examples: demonstrations, vigils, marches, letters to the editor, resolutions, press releases and/or press conferences, petition campaigns, lifestyle changes

Advocacy   Working through the legislative process or in the public square to impact public policy

Examples: meeting with public officials, writing letters to elected representatives, giving testimony at public hearings

Community Organizing   Participating in the process by which decisions that affect the community are made; this approach is based on the recognition that individuals have greater ability to change their situations when they participate in groups that know how to organize and influence power.

Examples: collaborating with local organizations, gathering neighbors in a community meeting, engaging in interfaith cooperation around justice issues

While it can be easy for adults to assume control of social action projects because they may have more experience with the issues at hand, engagement with social justice can be more meaningful when it comes directly from youth. Help your youth think through logistics and ensure that the planned activities are safe, but allow them to take the lead.

As a youth advisor, you can also hold up the religious relevance of social justice issues and encourage your youth to engage in spiritual reflection before and after a social action event. Debriefing after an intense event or experience can be especially helpful. Consider doing some "collective visioning" beforehand, in which each participant describes their vision of a more just and loving world, church, school, and community, and the youth can see where their visions overlap and intersect. The areas of intersection can be fruitful to engage with social action projects.

Social justice can also be a fabulous gateway to multigenerational cooperation across a congregation. Youth can inspire the entire church to help provide services for immigrant families or to advocate for support for the homeless in your community. Most congregational social justice committees or task forces would be ecstatic to have the youth approach them with their interests. Just make sure that the adults understand that collaborations are a two-way street!

Here are two excellent resources on youth social action, available through the UUA Bookstore:

Schwendeman, Jill. *When Youth Lead: A Guide to Intergenerational Social Justice Ministry (Plus 101 Youth Projects)*. Boston: Unitarian Universalist Association, 2007.

McAdoo, Jennifer, and Anne Principe. *Journeys of the Spirit: Planning and Leading Mission Trips with Youth*. Boston: Unitarian Universalist Association, 2010.

Finally, remember that each social justice project consists of three parts: understanding, acting, and reflecting. By starting with understanding, we recognize the limits of our current knowledge and experience. We try to comprehend the struggles that others face from their perspectives and learn about the broader context of the issues at hand. After the action itself, reflection allows space for youth to process what they have seen and done, and give voice to intense emotions they may feel. Reflection also brings a spiritual element to ground the social justice project in UU Principles and values.

Worship

Worship provides some of the most deeply meaningful experiences for UU youth and is a direct embodiment of UU principles and values. Providing the space and support for your youth to plan and lead worship services—from a simple ritual at a youth group meeting to a full-scale Sunday morning service—can be as satisfying and enriching for you as it is for them.

Experiencing a youth-style worship service, sometimes called "circle worship," may feel a bit different from a traditional adult service. Instead of a choir and organ, you may be singing hymns as chants or rounds. You might end up sitting on the floor or entering the worship space by holding hands. Instead of a sermon, youth worship generally places a ritual at the center of the service that explores the service's theme in an interactive way. Rituals are also wonderful ways to celebrate the milestones of adolescence. More information on Coming of Age and Bridging programs is available in the Religious Education chapter.

Although youth themselves should be the ones leading the planning process for their own worship services, you can support them in a number of ways, starting by familiarizing yourself with the elements of worship services. Here's a list of some of the most common worship elements:

Gathering and welcoming helps participants create a sacred space and find a worshipful mood, and demonstrates that all are welcome here.

Opening often includes a chalice lighting with accompanying words that set the theme for the service; it opens the time we choose to spend together as UUs.

Songs and hymns can be any type of religious or praise song; they can unite a group in a shared activity and raise or calm the energy of the community.

Readings give participants time to center themselves and reflect on the message and can include poetry, guided meditations, spoken song lyrics, or any other writings by youth or adults.

Giving includes announcements, joys and concerns, or offertories, and allows us to participate in the life of religious community by sharing the gift of our presence.

Receiving inspires, informs, and deepens the theme of the service through readings, homily, dance, poetry, or art.

Centerpiece the focal point of the service and its theme, could be a sermon for a Sunday morning service or a check-in for a weekly youth group; rituals are common centerpieces for youth services that can be borrowed from previous services or invented specifically for each service (for example, passing around a bowl of water, everyone dipping their hands in the water to represent something bad in their lives that they are washing off as well as something good they are taking in).

Closing   brings everyone together and officially marks the end of the worship through a short reading or a simple "blessed be"; it can be followed by a closing song or postlude.

If your youth are inexperienced with worship, you might find yourself choosing readings or songs at first, because building the confidence and skill of your youth in worship planning takes time. A wonderful variety of readings, chants, and songs can be found in the UU hymnals *Singing the Living Tradition, Singing the Journey,* and *Las voces del camino.*

You can encourage youth to think deeply and creatively about the themes they choose. Worship can center on any meaningful issue for youth. As an advisor, you can encourage your youth to carefully consider potential pitfalls such as cultural misappropriation, insensitivity, and exclusion. For example, rituals in which differently abled youth may not be able to take part might exclude some members from participating. Here's a list of common themes used in youth worship services:

- balance
- belonging
- circles
- cooperation
- death and life
- family issues
- freedom
- friendship
- gender

- healing
- home
- intergenerational sharing
- nature
- self-confidence
- self-respect
- stereotypes
- stewardship
- transitions

Once your youth feel more comfortable with worship, they might be interested in leading a Sunday morning worship service. This is a great way to showcase the talent of the youth in your congregation and to empower youth as multigenerational leaders. Youth often bring a refreshing and deeply spiritual touch to worship. If your youth are interested in doing a Youth Sunday service, make sure you help them reach out to the minister or Worship Committee so that they have a positive experience working with adults in the church. For these larger services in particular, setting up a realistic planning schedule can make all the difference by giving youth the time to put together an inspiring worship service.

If your youth group isn't used to worship or is really turned off by the idea, they might get inspired at a youth camp or conference. Worship is an important element of district conferences, and your youth group will see an excellent example of youth-led worship there. Many youth groups come back from conferences inspired to make worship a regular experience in their own group.

Learning

There probably isn't a youth group meeting in which someone doesn't learn something. Social action, leadership, worship—and even the most social of youth group gatherings—provide learning opportunities. In addition to the structured curricula available for high school-aged students, think about ways to weave spiritual exploration and development into every activity or event.

Youth groups are great places for discussion. You can bring in speakers to discuss issues about which youth are particularly interested. Ask a parishioner with a special skill or hobby to come and share it with the group. Youth groups have done everything from learning to sail to studying the history of Unitarian Universalism in Transylvania to developing their own photo exhibit. Find out what your group is interested in and what your congregation has to offer. Small group ministry approaches also offer structured discussions on spiritual issues. See the Religious Education chapter for more ideas.

Leadership

Youth leadership takes many forms, from being an elected or chosen leader of a youth group to heading up a project or serving on a church committee. However, youth leadership is always a shared endeavor with adults, and roles change and evolve as youth gain more leadership skills and independence. See the chapter on Youth in Leadership for more information.

Congregational Involvement

The final aspect of the Six Pillars of a Balanced Youth Program is congregational involvement, or creating space for the youth to share their gifts and participate in a multigenerational congregation. A good youth program will be a catalyst for creating relationships across generations in our congregations. Youth will thrive in their leadership development if they feel that they are empowered by the whole congregation, not just the youth advisor. Youth have talents, perspectives, and leadership skills that can be valuable in every aspect of congregational life.

Advisors can help make this happen in two ways. The first is to encourage youth to take part in the activities of the larger church. Many youth may not realize that they have something to offer the Worship Committee, but with your encouragement, they might help transform the way your congregation worships. You might encourage youth with musical talent to join the choir or the music ministry team. You can also advocate for youth with church leaders. As an adult, you can help open doors for youth participation and leadership by introducing youth to committee chairs, by encouraging committees to invite youth into their membership, and by asking adult leaders to include youth in planning programs and events for the church community.

Web of Youth Ministry

Another way to think of youth ministry is as an interconnected web. The Web of Youth Ministry expands the Six Pillars of a Balanced Youth Program to include new areas such as pastoral care and identity formation, and reframes youth ministry in more explicitly religious and faith development language. The Web of Youth Ministry arose from the changes in youth ministry that took place in the late 2000s through a reenvisioning process. (See the Reenvisioning Youth Ministry section of the Youth Ministry and You chapter.) It acknowledges that youth ministry extends beyond the traditional youth group setting, and that congregations should offer multiple pathways for youth to par-

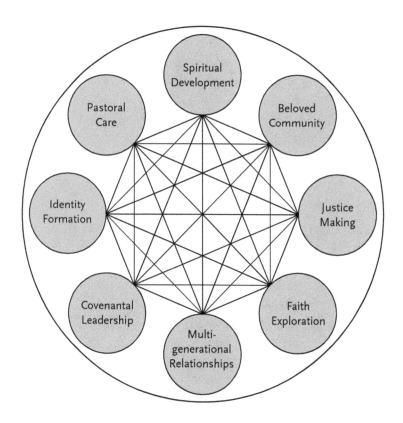

ticipate in and benefit from the ministry of our congregations. A brief description of the eight elements of the Web of Youth Ministry follows.

Spiritual Development

This is the intentional cultivation of spirituality through both individual and group spiritual practices. As spiritual beings, youth experience awe, gratitude, wonder, appreciation, and "at-one-ness." Youth ministry should encourage and offer opportunities for engagement in practices that nurture and enliven their spirits.

Beloved Community

Being held in the arms of a beloved community is an essential part of being a religious person of any age. In youth ministry, beloved community has three dimensions: local, Unitarian Universalist, and interfaith. Youth should be grounded in a local community that creates deep, affirming authentic and long-lasting relationships. Through camps and conferences, youth can connect with the wider Unitarian Universalist faith movement and see the diversity of experiences that exist within Unitarian Universalism. Interfaith community enriches youth ministry and celebrates differing religious perspectives found in the world.

Justice Making

Youth practice answering our faith's calling to work for justice and to be in solidarity with others who also work for justice in many settings, including in our lives, our local communities, and the wider world. Service trips can help open youth's eyes to the realities confronting other people and inspire them to work for justice. Organizing a social justice project within the congregation can connect youth to the rest of the congregation and place youth as leaders in the social justice work of the community. Youth can also engage in advocacy and education around social justice issues that are important to them.

Faith Exploration

Structured learning environments promote the free and responsible search for truth, meaning, and purpose as a part of youth faith development. Faith exploration takes place when youth engage with workshops at camps and conferences, as well as through curricula that challenge youth to look deep and develop their faith. See the Religious Education chapter for examples. Because the Unitarian Universalist approach to religious education acknowledges that we are all both learners *and* teachers, when youth are asked to lead or facilitate education programs, it is a learning *and* leadership development opportunity.

Multigenerational Relationships

Multigenerational faith communities have programs that both meet the specific developmental needs of different age groups and bring people together across age groups. Dynamic youth ministry strives to connect youth with people of all ages through inviting them to help with religious education programs, building mentor relationships between youth and adults, forming multigenerational choirs, allowing youth to use their leadership gifts in worship services and workshops, celebrating life milestones such as Coming of Age and Bridging into adulthood, and having fun outdoor retreats open to all families and ages.

Covenantal Leadership

Youth leadership is a covenantal practice in which youth are safe, recognized, and affirmed as full and vital participants in the life of our shared Unitarian Universalist faith community. Advisors encourage youth to take on more responsibility as they grow and develop. The goal is for youth to become empowered and effective leaders through intentional leadership development over time.

Identity Formation

Dynamic youth ministry supports youth in their journeys to figure out who they are as spiritual beings, relational beings, racial/ethnic and sexual beings, people of faith, justice makers, and lifelong learners and leaders, as well as how they fit in multigenerational communities. Youth ministry helps youth develop a healthy identity in these areas and learn to live with integrity so that their Unitarian Universalist faith is inseparable from their identity as a whole person.

Pastoral Care

Like people of all ages, youth have specific pastoral needs that are met in communities where people know how to listen deeply. Everyone works together to create a religious community that provides pastoral care with youth. This includes creating safe congregations, supporting youth who are in crisis, and celebrating their joys and accomplishments. Pastoral care with youth is also strengthened when ministers have a direct relationship with the youth in their congregations.

You may notice that, if not for the title, the Web of Youth Ministry could easily represent ministry for the whole congregation! This illustrates an important truth: Youth ministry is just as complex and important as ministry with the rest of the church. In fact, a strong youth ministry program is key to the future of any church, since it is the time when those who have grown up in the church are deciding whether to commit to lifelong participation.

Religious Education Programs

Religious education and theological exploration are part of any comprehensive faith development program, and youth programs are no exception. Even though your role as an advisor may or may not include being a teacher for religious education classes, you should know what types of religious education programs your youth are experiencing. If you are not a teacher or religious educator, your congregation's religious educator is probably already familiar with these curricula; as an advisor you should be in touch with that person to figure out how your programs can and should relate. The curricula described below include a range of programs for high school-aged youth, as well as some junior high materials that may be appropriate for younger youth groups.

Well-known programs such as Our Whole Lives and Coming of Age are common in UU churches, and are often the first hook for young high school students into the wonderful world of youth ministry. These programs are widely loved and recognized, but they require a large investment of time and energy on the part of the entire congregation. There are also other curricula available for youth that are easier to get started. If your youth group likes to write poetry, perhaps you can adapt a workshop from the Tapestry of Faith curriculum *Exploring Our Values Through*

Poetry. You can use religious education materials in a variety of ways to enhance your group or to collaborate with your church's religious education program, so use your imagination! Junior high, high school, and multigenerational curricula are included in this chapter so that you can have a sense of the breadth of resources that are available.

Our Whole Lives

Our Whole Lives (OWL) is a sexuality education program with curricula for all ages that models and teaches caring, compassion, respect, and justice. It is a holistic program that moves beyond the intellect to address the attitudes, values, and feelings that youth have about themselves and the world in an inclusive and developmentally appropriate manner. Participants build interpersonal skills and learn to understand the spiritual, emotional, and social aspects of sexuality. Jointly developed by the Unitarian Universalist Association and the United Church of Christ, the program and its underlying values reflect the justice-oriented traditions of both denominations.

The grade 7–9 curriculum is one of the most commonly used and offers a meaningful exploration of issues related to sexuality. For youth, a grade 10–12 curriculum is also available. Other curricula include grades K–1, grades 4–6, young adults, and adults. OWL teachers must also have completed facilitator training in order to purchase the curricula.

Coming of Age

For many youth, Coming of Age (COA) programs are the first formative experience of religious identity. These programs allow youth to explore their own theology, to connect with their UU history and community, and to share their journey with adults, mentors, and the entire congregation. They also often include major events at the end of the program, such as mission trips or pilgrimages to Boston and a Sunday morning service. Typically held for eighth or ninth graders, and sometimes offered only every other year because of the significant investment of staff time and resources they require, COA programs demonstrate that the congregation is committed to youth as part of the religious community.

COA programs can be wonderful gateways to youth group participation. Youth may leave the intense COA experience with a close-knit peer group and think, "This is great! What's next?" This group can be a captive audience for you as youth advisor, so think about how you can deliberately engage and recruit them for other aspects of youth ministry.

Coming of Age Handbook for Congregations by Rev. Sarah Gibb Millspaugh is a comprehensive and practical guide for adults who lead COA programs. This handbook provides workshops for youth, small group ministry sessions for parents, social action projects, and rites of passage. Participants explore theology, spirituality, history, and other topics through discussion, drama, music, writing, and art.

Bridging

Bridging: A Handbook for Congregations by Gail Forsyth-Vail and Jessica York offers adaptable resources and a blueprint for a year-long program leading to a ceremony to mark the transition from youth to young adulthood that complements the traditions and practices of your congregation. At the same time, it invites the congregation to deepen and strengthen its ministry to young adults beyond the bridging year.

Tapestry of Faith

Tapestry of Faith is a series of free online programs and resources for all ages that nurture Unitarian Universalist identity, spiritual growth, a transforming faith, and vital communities of justice and love. They are a core set of curricula available to religious educators that cover a wide range of issues and styles.

The following titles are available as of March 2012. Check the UUA website at www.uua.org/tapestry for more information about new programs and updates to previous ones.

High School

Virtue Ethics: An Ethical Development Program for High School Youth
Jessica York
We make hundreds of decisions every day. Some are small. Some are life changing, although we may not know their significance when we make them. This program's premise—in the words of the Buddha, recited in every workshop opening—is that "our thoughts and actions become habits and our habits shape our character." We have some control over our character. We can shape the person we want to be by making intentional, thoughtful decisions.

A Chorus of Faiths: Unitarian Universalists as Interfaith Leaders
Renee Ruchotzke and Hannah McConnaughay
Part of a joint venture of the UUA and the Interfaith Youth Core (founded by Eboo Patel) and funded by the Shelter Rock congregation, these sessions develop UU youth as interfaith leaders. Youth explore values of service to our community and religious pluralism through stories from our Sources and personal storytelling. They also coordinate an interfaith service project.

A Place of Wholeness
Beth Dana and Jesse Jaeger
Youth, like adults and children, need to be able to talk about what it means to be Unitarian Universalist. Whether delivering an "elevator speech," taking part in an interfaith dialogue, or conversing with friends at the lunch table, youth need practice describing our multifaceted faith in terms that are personally

meaningful and true. Building upon the faith development of Coming of Age and other UU identity programs, this curriculum encourages youth to look inward for a clearer understanding of their personal faith and guides them to express that faith outward into the world.

Exploring Our Values through Poetry
Karen Harris
This program utilizes poems that address elements of the spiritual life: acute observation, conscious and continuous inquiry, the unveiling of reality, hope and hopelessness, the afterlife, and the tenderness of the human condition.

Toolkit Book Supplement to Journeys of the Spirit: Planning and Leading Mission Trips with Youth
Jennifer McAdoo and Anne Principe
A supplement to the paperback manual in the Tapestry of Faith Toolkit series that inspires and guides youth advisors and youth leaders to create a spiritually transformative service project. Five useful sample forms for mission trip planning are available online as Word documents.

Junior High School

Heeding the Call: Qualities of a Justice Maker (Junior High School)
Nicole Bowmer and Jodi Tharan
Youth are encouraged to view themselves as agents of change in the world as they develop qualities crucial to justice work. They reflect on their own lives while making connections to the lives lived by others, building self-awareness while growing as leaders. It includes a Justice Makers Guide to help youth track their activities outside the workshop and a long-term Faith in Action project to lead youth, step-by-step, in becoming allies to marginalized communities.

Families
Helen Bishop and Susan Grider
A photo documentary curriculum which demonstrates that who
is in a family varies widely and contributes to healthy diversity.

Multigenerational

Gather the Spirit
Richard S. Kimball and Christine T. Rafal, Ed.D.
This is an eight-session, multigenerational program that teaches
stewardship, with a focus on water. Stewardship can take many
forms: donating money to our congregations and to causes
we care about; volunteering to teach, to lead, or to physically
maintain our congregations; helping to meet the needs of
others and protecting our shared resources in our local and
global communities.

Wisdom from the Hebrew Scriptures
Thomas R. Schade and Gail Forsyth-Vail
This program offers multigenerational workshops based on eight
stories from the Hebrew scriptures. Some of these stories are
well-known and others less so. Some have been told to children
in Sunday school classes and Hebrew school for generations;
others will be unknown even to some adults. Some of the narra-
tives fit well with contemporary Unitarian Universalist values and
others are more challenging in both the theology and the values
expressed. All of these stories offer wisdom that can help people
of all ages grow in spiritual depth and understanding.

Small Group Ministry

The small group ministry model of discussions within a congregation is a great format for senior high groups that enjoy
in-depth conversations. Sometimes known as covenant groups
or chalice circles, they provide a regular structured discussion
on spiritual and philosophical issues. Although often geared

toward adults, small group ministry can be an excellent venue for youth because it gives them the space to talk with one another about the challenges, thoughts, and joys in their lives, while still keeping liberal religious values present in the discussion. These groups can:

► Foster relationships within community

► Offer a spiritual setting for personal growth

► Allow group members to interact on a meaningful level

► Let everyone's voice be heard

► Provide entries into pastoral care systems for people in need

► Allow for flexible, open communities of varying size and composition

The UU Small Group Ministry Network is a good source for discussion guides and materials for facilitators (www.smallgroup-ministry.net).

One Tapestry of Faith curriculum is geared toward small group ministry:

Sharing the Journey: Small Group Ministry with Youth
Jessica York and Helen Zidowecki
Many of our congregations have embraced the use of small group ministry or covenant groups with adults. Small group ministry can be a way to help individuals build relationships, experience a greater sense of belonging, and feel supported in their spiritual journey in the congregation. Yet it is only beginning to be used with youth. We hope this resource will answer

questions and provide encouragement for congregations seeking new ways to engage Unitarian Universalist youth.

All the curricula described here are available for download at www. uua.org/re or for purchase through the Unitarian Universalist Association Bookstore at www.uuabookstore.org.

Supporting Youth Advisors

If your religious educator or minister gave you this guide, you might want to give it back so that person can read this chapter as well! Make sure that whoever recruited you has not just sent you off to be with the youth with no support other than this book. If you are a religious professional and youth ministry is a part of your portfolio, make sure your congregation understands what it takes to support your programs and is able provide the necessary volunteer advisors. During the reenvisioning process described in the Youth Ministry and You chapter, the Consultation on Youth Ministry found that youth advisors consistently felt unsupported and frustrated with their congregation's level of support and attention for youth ministry. Ministry with youth is a whole community effort, and should have the ongoing support of the religious educator, minister, Youth/Adult Committee, Religious Education Committee, parents, and Board of Trustees. They should all read this manual, or at least this chapter.

In the chapter Creating a Balanced Program, the Web of Youth Ministry demonstrated that good ministry to youth looks a lot like good ministry in any other context. However, it can be easy to forget that the constant negotiation and evaluation required of shared youth/adult leadership can actually take more effort than ministry to adults or children alone. Adolescence is a critical point in personal development, in which youth start to settle on the affiliations and identities they will hold for the rest of their lives. Churches able to establish strong youth programs stand a much better chance of staying connected to those youth once they become young adults.

Congregations should understand that it takes time to build up a strong youth ministry program, but few other investments can pay such rich dividends. Better support for youth, especially youth bridging into emerging adulthood, is crucial for retaining the wonderful youth leaders we grow in our churches.

Often, congregations are so relieved to find people willing to lead our youth groups that they forget the high-risk position in which we put our youth, advisors, and congregations when we don't provide adequate screening, training, supervision, and safety policies. Taking a few extra steps in each of these areas will ensure that we provide the safest experience possible for our youth.

Creating an Advising Team

No advisor should be working solo with youth. Youth groups need a team of competent, committed adults if they are to have the leadership and continuity they need to flourish. If you have more than one adult working with the youth group, each advisor can have a week off now and then when they need a break. And if one adult has to stop advising, the whole program doesn't come to a halt. One advisor trying to do it all will rapidly lead to advisor burnout.

Having more than one advisor is also helpful for the youth. Asking the entire youth group to relate to just one adult is often too limiting. If you have a team, each youth will be more likely to find at least one adult with whom to make a special connection. A team can provide a variety of perspectives and life experiences to draw from in group discussions. Moreover, getting more members of your congregation involved in youth programs is always a good idea. Adults can make assumptions about youth when they don't know them as individuals. The more the adults in your congregation are exposed to youth, the easier it will be to break down this prejudice.

Adults can assist in advising in ways other than working with a weekly youth group. They can be sponsors at conferences or for special field trips, and their time commitment can be as large or as limited as they like.

Great Recruitment Ideas

The process for recruiting advisors should involve input from the youth, the religious educator, the Youth/Adult Committee, if there is one, and the minister(s). You should hope to receive more applications than you need. As you build on your successes year after year, you will attract more adults who want to be a part of your vibrant youth program. Remember, adults who are not chosen as advisors can be involved in youth programs in other ways. Here are some suggestions to help you get as many qualified applicants as possible:

▶ *Ask!*
  Many people like to be asked, and they will appreciate your confidence in their ability. Others may not even be aware that an opportunity to advise the youth group exists unless you tell them about it. It's always easy to assume someone else will answer the call, but much harder to refuse when someone recruits you to be part of the team.

▶ *Be specific about your expectations*
  Prepare a job description so potential advisors know what they are committing to. They will be much more likely to agree if they know exactly what is expected of them and if the job isn't overwhelming.

▶ *Recruit more than one advisor*
Develop an advising team. People are more likely to agree if they know that all the work won't rest on their shoulders.

▶ *Ask church leaders for recommendations*
In a congregation that prioritizes multigenerational community, leaders will recognize that having competent youth advisors is central to the ministry of the church, just like the Caring Committee or the Annual Pledge Drive. Sometimes members of the Board of Trustees can help you recruit talented and capable church members.

▶ *Arrange a testimonial*
Have current advisors, youth, former advisors, and others testify from the pulpit about their positive experiences.

▶ *Take a survey*
Ask adults in the congregation what they would like to contribute to youth programs. Pass out a checklist that includes everything from baking cookies for a fundraiser to attending a conference to serving as a youth advisor. You probably will get many offers of help with the smaller jobs, but you also may find a couple of good candidates for youth group advisors.

▶ *Get more adults involved in smaller projects*
Help adults get their feet wet without making a long-term commitment. Once they get to know the youth, become interested in their lives, and feel less intimidated by them, they may volunteer for the bigger jobs. This strategy also helps with succession planning and getting adults into the pipeline for being advisors and youth allies.

▶ *Recruit parents*
Even though having parents as advisors can present some

problems if their children are also members of the youth group, they are often the people most interested in good youth programming for your church.

▶ *Pay your advisors*
Sometimes the extra income or a stipend can make the difference in convincing someone to commit to being a youth advisor, particularly for graduate students or people who are supporting themselves with several part-time jobs. Paying advisors also professionalizes the role and elevates the expectations of accountability. If you can't pay your advisors, make sure you at least have money budgeted so that their expenses for advising are reimbursed. It should not cost anyone anything to be an advisor!

▶ *Offer support*
Have a budget line item to provide advisors with resources such as this handbook, and books on games, activities, and leadership development. Send them to trainings, retreats, and other events at the church's expense.

Choosing Youth Group Advisors

Before recruiting, make sure you are clear about the procedure you will use to select your youth group advisors. It is recommended that both youth and adults be involved in the selection process. Once you've selected your advisors, establish a one- or two-month transition period (before the outgoing advisors are gone) to give the new advisor an opportunity to learn from the outgoing advisor and for the whole group to see if the arrangement is working well.

Ideally, each applicant should interview with the Youth/Adult Committee or an ad hoc committee of youth and adults established to select advisors. Check references, interview them, and make sure that they are a good fit for the youth group. Even if you know the applicants well, check references to get someone else's point of view. Make sure your advisors are a good fit for the goals of your congregation and your youth group. Some congregations require that an individual attend the congregation for at least six months before applying for a youth advisor position. If your congregation or youth group is committed to antiracism work, ask applicants about their experience with racial identity and antiracism work and let them know that they will be expected to participate in antiracism workshops. Finally, be sure to run criminal background checks on all adult advisors. See the Creating Safe Groups chapter for more information.

Training

Youth advisors will benefit from a training session geared specifically to them. Many districts and regions offer youth advisor trainings and webinars as well as general leadership training. They can include Chrysalis Youth Advisor trainings, which use curricula provided by the UUA to provide training specifically designed by UUA field staff and religious professionals for their district or area.

Once you have selected and trained your youth group advisors, don't leave them to flounder with no support. Establish regular meetings with your congregation's religious educator, Youth/Adult Committee, or Religious Education Committee.

Another excellent source of training for youth advisors is the Youth Ministry Renaissance Module. This is part of the series of trainings created for religious educators seeking professional religious education credentialing through the Unitarian Universalist Association. The module offers in-depth training on adolescent development and programming. For more information, visit www.uua.org/youth.

Contracts

A contract is a useful tool to help clarify what is expected of an advisor, even if you decide not to call it anything as formal as a contract. The document can spell out how many times an advisor will meet with the youth group each month, which expenses are reimbursable, how many weekend conferences or retreats the advisor is expected to attend each year, how often they will meet with the religious educator, what training and support the congregation will provide, how long the term as advisor will be, and other important information.

Make sure your contract includes the Code of Ethics for Adults Working With Youth. (See the Creating a Safe Group chapter.) Discuss what this code means with each advisor before that person signs the contract.

Contracts also delineate what financial compensation, if any, a youth advisor receives. Although paid youth staff may not be the norm in UU congregations, a small stipend for a dedicated part-time youth advisor may make the difference between burning out a volunteer or the ability to build a strong program over a few years. Information from the 2007 Consultation on Youth Ministry indicated that paid youth advisors felt more supported and empowered, and had better overall experiences compared to unpaid advisors.

Youth Programs for Our Future and Our Present

We all know that the youth of today are the adults of tomorrow. Youth who have valuable youth group experiences and identify as Unitarian Universalists throughout their teen years are more likely to stay in the movement. By contributing to youth ministry, you contribute directly to the future of Unitarian Universalism.

Our future world benefits from helping today's youth to be caring, concerned, and committed. What we strive for in our congregations and our lives is a future with peace, justice, human dignity, and genuine concern for others. These young people with whom you are choosing to spend your time will determine what the future looks like in your congregation, community, and world.

And our youth are not only our future; they have important insights and perspectives for our faith right now. This vision of a multigenerational faith has inspired youth, adults, volunteers, and religious professionals across the country. As an advisor, you are in a unique position to help integrate Unitarian Universalist youth into the life of our faith so that other adults can receive the gifts our youth have to offer. The more deeply connected our youth are with our congregations, our districts, and our Association, the more likely they are to stay involved as adults.

Please remember that the suggestions in this manual on how to provide Unitarian Universalist youth with the best possible programming are only ideas and jumping-off points. You can and will do it differently. Every congregation, district, youth group, and individual youth has its own needs, and there is no one right way to be a youth group advisor.

Above all, advisors need to be themselves, to model for youth how to navigate the world with authenticity, how to live out their Unitarian Universalist values, and how to seek their highest potential. If you set a good example, there is a good chance the youth will follow it. Be honest and genuine with the youth you advise, and they will love and trust you. You may have some of the best experiences of a lifetime too.

Resources

This section contains a number of resources to assist in your youth ministry planning and programming. Here you'll find some suggested projects that your youth group can do together. Also included are a copy of the UUA Code of Ethics for youth in leadership positions and the Participant Covenant for all youth and adult attendees, which were created to establish clear boundaries and expectations at UUA youth events and are good models for developing similar documents for your group. A list of websites, email lists, and other contact information is also provided to help you learn about more ways to offer effective youth ministry. Finally, a recommended reading list identifies books, reports, and handbooks related to youth ministry; many of these titles are available from the UUA Bookstore: www.uua-bookstore.org.

Project Ideas

These three project ideas are great suggestions for a congregational youth group of any size. They offer examples of how to integrate the elements described in both of the models outlined in the Creating a Balanced Program chapter. Each description below lists which of the elements from both the Six Pillars of Balanced Youth Programs and the Web of Youth Ministry are addressed by the project. You are free to use these ideas directly or to use them as inspiration for your own exciting project.

Congregational History Project

Pillars   Learning, Leadership, Congregational Involvement

Web   Beloved Community, Covenantal Leadership, Multigenerational Relationships, Faith Exploration

Youth can interview members of the congregation to create an oral history of the church. It's a great project for an anniversary year or other milestone in your congregation's life, but this project can also be done at any time! At its most basic, it requires individual and group conversations between youth and adult members of the congregation. In some settings, youth may be interviewing founding members. In others, elders are the focus.

Perhaps they are interviewing families involved in the Religious Education program or new members who have recently signed the membership book. Youth interviewers might ask them to share stories about their experiences in the congregation, their beliefs, or what drew them to Unitarian Universalism or the particular congregation. Some other examples of what to ask include:

▶ Ask founding members to tell stories about the founding of the congregation.

▶ Interview elders and ask how Unitarian Universalism (or their relationship to it) has changed over the years.

▶ Interview new members about what brought them to the congregation.

There's also a decision to be made about what to do after the interviews. You could:

▶ Create a photo display of pictures of the interviewees and their answers.

▶ Videotape the interviews and put together a short video.

▶ Collect documents and artifacts from the church's history to enrich photos and video displays.

▶ Create a book of stories. If you bind it at a print/copy center, you can sell it as a youth group fundraiser. Just make sure to get permission to print/use stories.

Consider asking the adults participating in the project to interview the youth as well.

Multigenerational Social Justice/Service Project

Pillars   Justice and Service, Leadership, Learning (depending on the project, also Worship)

Web   Justice Making, Beloved Community, Covenantal Leadership, Identity Formation (depending on the project, also Faith Exploration and Spiritual Development)

Social justice projects offer a variety of ways to connect youth with other ages and generations in the congregations. Start by having youth pick a justice issue on which they would like to focus. Before deciding on the action they want to take, they can learn about the issue to understand its context. For example, if their concern is hunger, before serving at a soup kitchen, participating in a drive for a food pantry, or collecting money for Heifer International, they can:

1. explore the causes of hunger, both domestically and internationally;

2. learn about who is affected, and challenge their own assumptions and stereotypes about who needs help;

3. decide what kind of action they want to take. They should consider why we engage in justice work as Unitarian Universalists in a way that is grounded in our principles and values.

In planning the project action, youth can either do the project within the youth group or invite other members of the congregation to participate. Projects can be short, one-day events. Others may be weekly commitments for a particular period of time. If your project is focused on youth participation rather than a multigenerational project, you might have additional options, such as taking a week-long service learning trip. For longer trips or experiences, consider how the group might reflect during the experience and stay grounded. Daily reflection groups? Morning worship before heading to work?

After doing a project, the group should have an opportunity to reflect on its experiences. This might happen in small group ministry circles, large group conversation, individual journaling prompts, or some other manner. Projects with participants of different ages offer youth a great opportunity to lead these follow-up discussions in multigenerational spaces. If youth are the only ones involved in the project action, they can bring a multigenerational lens to the project by sharing what they learned in worship with the rest of the congregation.

Possible partnerships include other local faith communities. This can be an exciting way for youth to interact with peers who come from different religious backgrounds. If you have a Social Action Team in your congregation, the youth can approach them about partnering on the project.

Community Fair

Pillars Leadership (depending on topic, also Justice and Service, Congregational Involvement, and/or Learning)

Web Covenantal Leadership, Beloved Community (depending on topic, also Faith Exploration, Justice Making, and/or Identity Formation)

This project involves opening the congregation to the wider community for a fair organized around a particular topic, interest, or need. Youth would choose the issue, identify who should be invited, and organize the logistics of the event, perhaps taking place on a Sunday afternoon following worship services.

Some ideas for such gatherings include:

▶ A fair for sexual and gender identity issues might feature a speaker supporting lesbian, gay, bisexual, transgender, and queer (LGBTQ) youth; tables for organizations such as the local Parents, Families, and Friends of Lesbians and Gays (PFLAG) chapter, the congregation's Interweave chapter, and any state or local groups that support LGBTQ individuals; information on LGBTQ rights issues in the state; and social opportunities, particularly for LGBTQ youth, LGBTQ elders, or LGBTQ parents.

▶ A fair for economic justice might feature tables from agencies that provide support and services to under- and unemployed people regarding job searches, housing support, low-cost medical care, worker organizing, and more. It could also include free childcare so that parents can attend.

▶ A more carnival-like event could double as a fundraiser, offering family-friendly activities, booth games, art stations, face painting, and more.

▶ An interfaith youth social could feature an open mic/coffeehouse, a drop-in service project for a local organization, stations to learn about one another's faith tradition, games, and food.

▶ Hosting a speaker on a particular issue of interest can appeal to the whole community, and related groups and organizations can be invited for connection and more information before or after the presentation. A presentation on immigration issues in the community, for example, could be coupled with a mini-fair of immigrant support organizations, advocacy groups, and legal support.

Some of these ideas require the whole congregation to be involved. Others can be done just by the youth. Most importantly, do something that the group is passionate about and work in good faith with the necessary partners.

UUA Code of Ethics for Youth in Leadership Positions

This paragraph is added to youth event forms and materials when appropriate.

Youth in leadership positions are uniquely visible and influential in any conference community. They are expected to recognize that power imbalances exist in their interactions with other participants. Sexual behavior with participants during the event is never acceptable; additionally, youth leaders should remain aware of the impact of their actions and behave accordingly. Youth who abuse their roles as leaders, consciously or not, can damage individuals and the community. Youth leaders are expected to use their influence in a positive manner.

Participant Covenant for UUA Youth Events

This covenant was developed specifically for UUA youth events. Each group or event is encouraged to develop its own covenant to respect appropriate safety boundaries.

Policy on Sexuality and Community for All Participants

While sexuality is a healthy and important part of young people's lives, there are times and places where sexual behavior is inappropriate. This policy seeks to create a healthy and safe space for all participants. Exclusive relationships detract from the community. All participants must abide by the following policies:

▶ Participants must respect each other's physical boundaries.

▶ Participants shall refrain from sexual, seductive, or erotic behavior while at the event.

▶ Sexual behavior between participants at the event and sexual harassment are not permitted and will not be tolerated.
Any harassment regarding race, color, national origin, religion,

age, sex, gender, sexual orientation, or disability will not be tolerated. Such harassment includes unsolicited remarks, gestures or physical contact, and display or circulation of written materials or derogatory pictures directed at any of these categories. In addition, sexual advances, jokes, explicit or offensive pictures, requests for sexual favors, sexting, and other verbal or physical conduct of a sexual nature constitute sexual harassment.

▶ The event leadership team is responsible for ensuring this policy is enforced. Parents/guardians are invited to discuss this policy with youth.

Code of Ethics for Adults

Adults who work with youth are in positions of power and play a key role in the spiritual and identity development of younger members of the community. Therefore, it is especially important that adults be qualified to provide the special nurture, care, and support that will enable youth to develop a healthy, positive sense of self and responsibility. Youth and adults suffer damaging effects when adults become sexually involved with young persons in their care; therefore, adults will not engage in any physical, sexual, seductive, erotic, or romantic behavior with youth. Neither shall they sexually harass or engage in behavior with youth which constitutes verbal, emotional, or physical abuse. In cases of violation of this code, appropriate action will be taken.

Behavioral Guidelines for Participants

▶ Respect the Policy on Sexuality and Community and Code of Ethics for Adults above.

▶ No drugs, weapons, or alcohol.

- No pets.

- All participants will remain on-site during the event.

- Adults must remain in the role of advisor at all times.

- Participants must abide by all applicable federal, state, and local laws.

- Participants must provide all requested, signed permission and release forms.

I have read and agree to adhere to these policies and guidelines while at the event. I understand that breach of this covenant will result in disciplinary action up to and including dismissal from the event and the inability to attend future UUA Youth events.

Name _____

Signature _____

Date _____

For More Information

Unitarian Universalist Association

www.uua.org

Office of Youth and Young Adult Ministries

www.uua.org/youth
The Office of Youth and Young Adult Ministries provides leadership, coordination, resources and materials, and advocacy for UU youth, young adult, and campus ministries. Call 617–948–4350 or email youth@uua.org for information regarding:

▶ Youth leadership development

▶ Social justice projects and trips

▶ Multigenerational congregations

▶ Identity-based youth ministry (race, gender and sexual identity, ability, etc.)

- Social media resources

- General Assembly Youth Caucus

- Bridging and transitions into young adulthood

- Any other youth ministry questions

Check out the Office's blog at blueboat.blogs.uua.org.

District and Regional Staff

www.uua.org/directory/districts
Based in five regions and nineteen districts, the UUA's field staff members are great resources. They should be your first call when you have questions! Find out who the contact is in your area by visiting www.uua.org/directory/districts or sending an email to: conglife@uua.org.

UUA Email Lists

www.lists.uua.org
These email discussion and announcement groups connect religious leaders, volunteers, and professionals across the denomination.

ADVISOR-L   A discussion list for youth advisors
LREDA-L   A discussion list for members of the Liberal Religious Educators Association
REACH-L   A discussion and sharing list for issues related to Unitarian Universalist religious education (no membership required)
PYMS-L   A discussion list for paid youth ministry staff

Recommended Reading

For Youth Ministry Advisors

Chow, David. *No More Lone Rangers: How to Build a Team-Centered Youth Ministry.* Loveland, CO: Group Publishing, 2003.

Dean, Kenda Creasy, and Ron Foster. *The Godbearing Life: The Art of Soul Tending for Youth Ministry.* Nashville: Upper Room Books, 1998.

DeVries, Mark. *Sustainable Youth Ministry: Why Most Youth Ministry Doesn't Last and What Your Church Can Do About It.* Downers Grove, IL: InterVarsity Press, 2008.

Fields, Doug. *Your First Two Years in Youth Ministry: A Personal and Practical Guide to Starting Right.* Grand Rapids, MI: Zondervan, 2002.

Gale, Greg. *Growing Together: A Guide for Building Inspired, Diverse, and Productive Youth Communities.* Lincoln, MA: The Food Project, 2006.

Hurd, Tracey. *Nurturing Children and Youth: A Developmental Guidebook.* Boston: Unitarian Universalist Association, 2005.

McAdoo, Jennifer, and Anne Principe. *Journeys of the Spirit: Planning and Leading Mission Trips with Youth.* Boston: Unitarian Universalist Association, 2010.

Rydberg, Denny. *Building Community in Youth Groups: Practical Models for Transforming Your Group into a Close, Caring Family.* Loveland, CO: Group Publications, 1985.

Schwendeman, Jill. *When Youth Lead: A Guide to Intergenerational Social Justice Ministry (Plus 101 Youth Projects).* Boston: Unitarian Universalist Association, 2007.

Yaconelli, Mark. *Growing Souls: Experiments in Contemplative Youth Ministry.* Grand Rapids, MI: Zondervan, 2007.

Additional Reading

Arnason, Wayne, and Rebecca Scott. *We Would Be One: A History of UU Youth Movements.* Boston: Skinner House Books, 2005.

Erslev, Kate Tweedie. *Full Circle: Fifteen Ways to Grow Lifelong UUs.* Boston: Unitarian Universalist Association, 2004.

Essex Conversations Coordinating Committee. *Essex Conversations: Visions for Lifespan Religious Education.* Boston: Skinner House Books, 2001.

Lerner, Richard M. *The Good Teen: Rescuing Adolescence from the Myths of the Storm and Stress Years.* New York: Stonesong Press, 2007.

Meacham, Denis. *The Addiction Ministry Handbook: A Guide for Faith Communities.* Boston: Skinner House Books, 2004.

Merritt, Carol Howard. *Tribal Church: Ministering to the Missing Generation.* Herndon, VA: The Alban Institute, 2007.

Patel, Eboo. *Acts of Faith: The Story of an American Muslim, the Struggle for the Soul of a Generation.* Boston: Beacon Press, 2007.

Patton, Sally. *Welcoming Children with Special Needs: A Guidebook for Faith Communities.* Boston: Unitarian Universalist Association, 2004.

Searl, Edward. *Coming of Age: A Treasury of Poems, Quotations and Readings on Growing Up.* Boston: Skinner House Books, 2006.

Tatum, Beverly Daniel. *Why Are All the Black Kids Sitting Together in the Cafeteria?* New York: Basic Books, 1997.

Young, Karen S., and Jenny Sazama. *15 Points: Successfully Involving Youth in Decision Making.* Somerville, MA: Youth on Board, 2006.

Program Books

Forsyth-Vail, Gail, and Jessica York. *Bridging: A Handbook for Congregations.* Boston: Unitarian Universalist Association, 2012.

Goldfarb, Eva S., and Elizabeth M. Casparian. *Our Whole Lives: Sexuality Education for Grades 10–12.* Boston: Unitarian Universalist Association and the United Church Board of Homeland Ministries, 2000.

Hoertdoerfer, Patricia, and Fredric Muir. *The Safe Congregation Handbook: Nurturing Healthy Boundaries in Our Faith Communities.* Boston: Unitarian Universalist Association, 2005.

Millspaugh, Sarah Gibb. *Coming of Age Handbook for Congregations.* Boston: Unitarian Universalist Association, 2009.

Wilson, Pamela M. *Our Whole Lives: Sexuality Education for Grades 7–9.* Boston: Unitarian Universalist Association and the United Church Board of Homeland Ministries, 1999.

UUA Reports and Materials

ConTemplate: PNWD YRUU Conference Planning Handbook. Boston: Pacific Northwest District, Unitarian Universalist Association, 2008.

Mosaic Project Report: An Assessment of Unitarian Universalist Ministry to Youth and Young Adults of Color and Latina/o and Hispanic and Multiracial/Multiethnic Descent. Boston: Unitarian Universalist Association, 2009.

Youth Ministry Working Group: Recommendations for Youth Ministry. Boston: Unitarian Universalist Association, 2009.

UUA Office of Youth and Young Adult Ministries

The Office of Youth and Young Adult Ministries connects leaders, equips congregations, and engages youth and young adults in promoting dynamic, multicultural, and multigenerational ministry. Serving youth (high school aged) and young adults (18–35), the Office provides resources to support healthy ministry and advocates for the voices and interests of youth and young adults across the Association. The Office's primary programs include:

- ▶ the Youth Caucus and the Young Adult Caucus of General Assembly

- ▶ regular social media presence and online communication, including Blue Boat, a blog of youth and young adult ministries

- ▶ campus ministry support and coordination

- ▶ information and materials for youth and young adults engaged in ministry in their own communities

▶ coordination and collaboration with other UUA offices, committees, and related groups

▶ grants, awards, and recognition for outstanding youth and young adult ministry

The Office can be reached by phone: 617–948–4350, or by email: youth@uua.org. Or you can visit us online: www.uua.org/youth.